In memory of my bubbe Zelda,

and for my daughters, Zelda and Billie

In honor of all the Jewish women of Poland

who resisted the Nazi regime

Warsaw with a weeping face,
with graves on street corners,
will outlive her enemies,
will still see the light of days.

From "A Chapter of Prayer," a song dedicated to the Warsaw ghetto uprising that won first prize in a song contest. Written by a young Jewish girl before her death, published in Women in the Ghettos, *1946.*

THE LIGHT OF DAYS

THE UNTOLD STORY OF WOMEN RESISTANCE FIGHTERS IN HITLER'S GHETTOS

JUDY BATALION

with Winifred Conkling

HARPER

An Imprint of HarperCollins

Library of Congress Control Number: 2020937196
ISBN 978-0-06-303770-0

Typography by Erin Fitzsimmons
22 23 24 25 26 PC/BRR   10 9 8 7 6 5 4 3 2 1

❖

First trade paperback edition, 2022

CONTENTS

WHO'S WHO
(IN ORDER OF APPEARANCE)

Renia Kukiełka: born in Jędrzejów, a courier for Freedom in Będzin.

Sarah Kukiełka: Renia's older sister, a Freedom member who takes care of Jewish orphans in Będzin.

Zivia Lubetkin: a Freedom leader in the Jewish Fighting Organization and in the Warsaw ghetto uprising.

Frumka Płotnicka: born in Pinsk, a Freedom member who leads the fighting organization in Będzin.

Hantze Płotnicka: (pronounced in English as *Han*-che) Frumka's younger sister, also a Freedom leader and courier.

Chajka Klinger: (pronounced in English as *Hay*-ka) a leader of The Young Guard and the fighting organization in Będzin.

Gusta Davidson: a courier and leader of Akiva, based in Kraków.

Hela Schüpper: a courier for Akiva, based in Kraków.

Irena Adamowicz: a Catholic woman who worked with the Polish underground and helped the Jewish underground. Code name: Zosia.

Bela Hazan: a Freedom courier, based in Grodno, Vilna, Białystok. Worked with couriers Lonka Kozibrodska and Tema Schneiderman.

Ruzka Korczak: (pronounced in English as *Rush*-ka) a leader of The Young Guard in Vilna's fighting organization and a partisan leader in the forests.

Vitka Kempner: a leader of The Young Guard in Vilna's fighting organization and a partisan leader in the forests.

Faye Schulman: a photographer who becomes a partisan nurse and fighter.

Anna Heilman: an assimilated Warsaw Young Guard member who takes part in the resistance at Auschwitz.

Poland in WWII

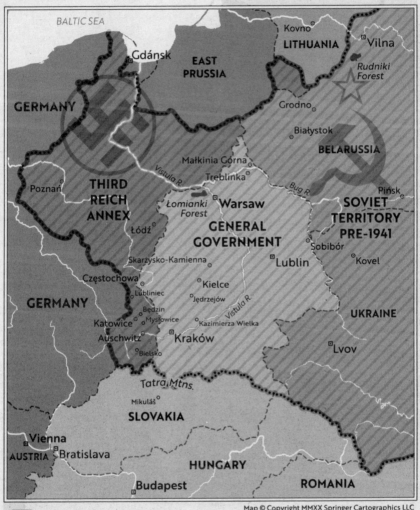

BALTIC SEA

GERMANY

EAST PRUSSIA

Gdánsk

LITHUANIA

Kovno

Vilna

Rudniki Forest

Grodno

Białystok

BELARUSSIA

Poznań

THIRD REICH ANNEX

Vistula R.

Małkinia Gorna

Treblinka

Bug R.

Pińsk

SOVIET TERRITORY PRE-1941

Łódź

Łomianki Forest

Warsaw

GENERAL GOVERNMENT

Kovel

Skarzysko-Kamienna

Sobibór

Lublin

Częstochowa

Kielce

Jędrzejów

Vistula R.

UKRAINE

Lubliniec

Będzin

Mysłowice

Kazimierza Wielka

Katowice

Auschwitz

Kraków

Lvov

Bielsko

GERMANY

Tatra Mtns.

Mikuláš

SLOVAKIA

Vienna

Bratislava

AUSTRIA

HUNGARY

Budapest

ROMANIA

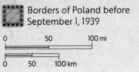

Borders of Poland before September 1, 1939

0   50   100 mi

0   50   100 km

INTRODUCTION

In the spring of 2007, I lived in London and worked as an art historian by day and a comedian by night. I was writing a play about strong Jewish women, and I wanted to learn more about Hannah Senesh, one of the few female resisters in World War II who was not lost to history. As a child, I read about Hannah and how, as a twenty-two-year-old, she joined the British paratroopers fighting the Nazis and went to Europe to help the resistance. She was captured but remained courageous to the end, refusing a blindfold at her own execution. Hannah faced the truth, lived and died for her convictions, and took pride in openly being just who she was.

I went to the British Library, looking for information about Hannah. There weren't many books about her, so I asked the research librarian for any that mentioned her name in the catalog. When the books arrived, the one on the bottom caught my eye; it was hardbacked and bound in a worn blue fabric with golden lettering on the cover. I opened it first and found nearly two hundred sheets of tiny script—in Yiddish. It was a language I knew but hadn't used in more than fifteen years. I almost returned it, but my curiosity urged me on.

I picked up *Freuen in di Ghettos* (*Women in the Ghettos*), published in New York in 1946, and flipped through the pages. Hannah was only mentioned in the last chapter. Before that, a hundred and seventy pages were filled with stories of other women—dozens of unknown young Jews who fought in the resistance against the Nazis, mainly from inside the ghettos.

These "ghetto girls" were fearless. They paid off Gestapo guards, hid revolvers in loaves of bread, and helped build systems of underground bunkers. They flirted with Nazis, bought them off with wine, whiskey, and pastry, and—when they had the chance—they shot and killed them without apology. These women carried out espionage missions, distributed fake IDs and underground flyers, and shared the truth about what was happening to the Jewish people. They helped the sick and taught the children; they bombed German train lines and blew up at least one city's electric supply. They helped Jews escape the ghettos through canals and chimneys, by digging holes in walls and crawling across rooftops. They bribed executioners, wrote underground radio bulletins, upheld group morale, and tricked the Gestapo into carrying their luggage filled with weapons.

I had never read anything like this. I had no idea that so many Jewish women had been involved in the resistance effort. These writings touched me personally, upending my understanding of my own history. I come from a family of Polish-Jewish Holocaust survivors. My bubbe Zelda did not fight in the resistance. She—who did not look Jewish with her high cheekbones and pinched nose—fled occupied Warsaw, swam across rivers, hid in a convent, flirted with a Nazi who turned a blind eye, and was transported in a truck carrying oranges across the Russian border. My bubbe lost her parents and three of her four sisters, all of whom remained in Warsaw. It was her successful but tragic escape story that shaped my understanding of survival.

My bubbe shared pieces of this dreadful story every afternoon as she babysat me after school, tears and fury in her eyes. The community where I lived in Montreal, Canada, was made up of Holocaust survivor families, who shared similar stories of pain and suffering.

When I was doing this research, for the first time I learned a different version of the women-in-war story. These women acted with daring. They were proud of their contributions to the war—smuggling, sabotaging, fighting, and gathering intelligence. They were fierce and fearsome, brave and brazen.

My bubbe was my hero, but what if she had decided to risk her life by staying and fighting? I was haunted by the question: What would I do in a similar situation? Would I have chosen to fight or tried to flee to safety?

Once I began to look, I discovered many more extraordinary tales of female fighters in the resistance. I found accounts in archives, memoirs published by museums, and hundreds of testimonies written in Polish, Russian, Hebrew, Yiddish, German,

French, Dutch, Danish, Greek, Italian, and English, from the 1940s to today.

Holocaust scholars have debated what counts as an act of Jewish resistance. Some define "resistance" as any action that affirmed the humanity of a Jew or defied Nazi policy, including simply staying alive. Other academics feel that such a general definition fails to recognize those who risked their lives to actively defy the regime. These scholars make a distinction between *resistance* and *resilience*.

The rebellious acts that I discovered among Jewish women in Poland—my country of focus—include both types. For many, the goal was to rescue Jews; for others, it was to die with dignity and self-respect. The female "ghetto fighters" often came from Jewish youth group movements. These young women were combatants, editors of underground bulletins, and social activists. Many were "couriers," who disguised themselves as non-Jews and traveled between locked ghettos and towns, smuggling people, cash, documents, information, and weapons.

Months into my research, I had collected more stories than I had ever expected to find. How would I possibly narrow it down?

Ultimately, as in *Women in the Ghettos*, I focused on female ghetto fighters from the youth movements "Freedom" and "The Young Guard." The centerpiece of the Yiddish book is an account written by a female courier who signed her name "Renia K." I was drawn to Renia because she was a savvy, middle-class girl who happened to find herself in the middle of a nightmare. Renia rose to the occasion, fueled by anger and an inner sense of justice. Later, I learned that Renia had written a memoir in Polish that was translated and published in Hebrew in 1945. An English translation was published in 1947, but it was largely forgotten. I hope to propel her story—as well as the stories of other women—from the background to the forefront, celebrating and recognizing these Jewish women who displayed acts of astonishing bravery.

This is not a story of underdog victory. The Polish-Jewish resistance movement only had limited military success. But success cannot be measured by Nazi casualties or the number of Jews saved alone.

The resistance effort was larger and more organized than most people realize. Jewish armed underground groups operated in more than ninety eastern European ghettos. Uprisings took place in Warsaw as well as in other Polish cities and villages, including Będzin, Vilna, Białystok, Kraków, Lvov, Częstochowa, Sosnowiec, and Tarnów. Armed Jewish rebellions broke out in at least five major concentration and death camps—including Auschwitz, Treblinka, and Sobibor—as well as in eighteen forced labor camps. Jewish networks financially supported twelve thousand Jews-in-hiding in Warsaw.

Why had I not heard these stories? Why had I not heard about the hundreds, even thousands, of Jewish women who were involved in every aspect of this rebellion? Why wasn't *Women in the Ghettos* a classic on Holocaust reading lists?

I came to learn that there have been many factors—both personal and political—that have determined which parts of Holocaust history have endured. For many, silence has been a way of coping; remembering the horrors is simply too painful. Even when storytellers have shared their resistance stories, there has been little focus on women. In the rare cases where writers have included females in their tales, these women are often portrayed as minor figures and girlfriends rather than as leaders. In fact, women were uniquely suited to some crucial and life-threatening tasks, such as working as couriers.

When *Women in the Ghettos* was written, many contributors assumed that the women in the book would be recognized as the heroes they were. Seventy-five years later, these names remain largely unknown, their page in the book of eternal memory unwritten. Until now.

PART ONE

Ghetto Girls

"Is someone needed . . . to smuggle in contraband such as illegal publications, goods, money? The girls volunteer as though it were the most natural thing in the world. . . . How many times have they looked death in the eyes? How many times have they been arrested and searched? . . . The story of the Jewish woman will be a glorious page in the history of Jewry during the present war."

—Emanuel Ringelblum, diary entry, May 1942

ONE

Here, We Stay

October 1924

On Friday, October 10, as the Jews in the small Polish town of Jędrzejów (pronounced YEN-jeh-yuf in Polish) were shutting their shops and preparing for the Sabbath—a day of religious observance—Moshe Kukiełka rushed from his store. His small stone home was on the main road, just around the bend from a magnificent medieval abbey. As sunset approached, the orange autumn light flooded the lush valleys and rolling hills around them. As a Jew, Moshe was used to hurrying home before sunset on Fridays for the Shabbat meal and prayers, but on this night, he had another reason to rush. His wife was expecting a baby.

When Moshe arrived home, he met his third daughter and immediately fell in love. He and his wife, Leah, named the baby Rivka in Hebrew. In the Bible, Rivka was one of the four matriarchs of the Jewish people. The baby also had a Polish name: Renia.

It was 1924, just one year after Poland's borders were finalized following years of occupation. The economy was stable, and Moshe ran a successful small business, selling buttons, clothing, and sewing supplies. He raised a middle-class family—Renia had older siblings: Sarah, Zvi, and Bela—and exposed them to music and literature. At the Shabbat table that week, the family enjoyed ginger cake, chopped liver with onions, potato and sweet noodle pudding, plums and apples, and tea.

As Moshe held his daughter, he had no idea what was to come. Still, as he looked down at his little Renia, with her big green eyes, light brown hair, and delicate face, he may have realized she was special. She was born to make a difference in the world.

Renia's hometown of Jędrzejów was a small Polish market town, about half Jewish and half Christian. Jews had been allowed to settle in the region since the 1860s. Most Jews worked as peddlers and small-business owners with shops near the market square. The rest were mainly artisans, such as shoemakers, bakers, and carpenters. The majority of Jews in Jędrzejów lived in poverty, but about 10 percent were wealthy and owned timber mills, flour mills, and mechanical workshops as well as property on the main square.

Across Poland, modern Jewish culture flourished in the early 1930s. Jewish newspapers, magazines, and bookstores thrived. Renia's father helped feed the poor and tend to the dead by supporting the local burial organization. He served as a cantor in his synagogue. He was a Zionist; he believed that Jews could only live freely and openly in a homeland of their own in Palestine. Poland may have been home to his ancestors for a thousand years, but that was temporary. Moshe hoped to one day move his family to "the promised land."

Renia's parents valued education. There were a number of Jewish schools in Jędrzejów, but religious education was costly and often reserved for sons only. Renia attended Polish public school. She was at the top of her class of thirty-five. She had Catholic friends and spoke fluent Polish in the schoolyard. She didn't realize it at the time, but this exposure to Polish culture and language became critical training for her work in the resistance; she learned to speak Polish without a Jewish-sounding accent.

Even so, Renia was not fully accepted by her Polish classmates. At a ceremony when she was called up to receive an academic award, a classmate threw a pencil case at her forehead because she was Jewish. She was neither "in" nor "out."

Renia likely joined her beloved father at readings, talks, and political rallies. At the time, Zionist Jews debated the question of belonging. How did they fit in? They had lived in Poland for centuries, but they were never considered truly Polish. Were they Polish first or Jewish first? These questions were becoming more important due to the rise in antisemitism, or anti-Jewish attitudes, across Europe.

The "Polish-Jewish identity" question had been going on for centuries. Medieval Jews had migrated to Poland because it was a safe haven from countries in western Europe, where they were persecuted and expelled. They were relieved to arrive in this tolerant land with economic opportunity. "Po-Lin," the Hebrew name for the country, actually means "here, we stay." For Jews at that time, Poland offered relative freedom and safety, a place to build a future.

But the Polish people didn't fully embrace their Jewish neighbors. Religious tolerance was made law as far back as the 1573 Warsaw Confederation, but the Jews still felt threatened. Poles were resentful of Jews' economic freedom, in particular, practices that permitted Jews to become landlords and conduct business activities that the church did not allow Poles to engage in. In the late 1700s, the Polish government was unstable, and the country was invaded by Germany, Austria, and Russia, then divided into three parts, each ruled by a captor who imposed their own customs. The Polish people maintained their language and literature, but the country was not reunited until 1918.

Once united, Poland needed to rebuild both its cities and

its identity. A patriotic, pro-Poland movement spread. Many of the leaders blamed Polish Jews for causing the country's poverty and problems. These people believed that a Jew could never be a Pole. Generations of living in Poland made no difference.

The democratic government was unstable. When Renia was eleven, the right-wing nationalists took over. Almost overnight, conditions became much harder for the Jews. While the government didn't support direct violence, it did encourage boycotts of Jewish businesses. The Catholic Church condemned Nazi racism but tolerated anti-Jewish sentiment. At universities, Polish students championed German chancellor Adolf Hitler, who imposed laws that discriminated against Jews. His goal was to eliminate all Jews from Germany. In Poland, Jewish students were forced to sit at the back of lecture halls as second-class students.

Renia and her family saw increasing antisemitism in Jędrzejów during the late 1930s. Racial slurs became common, and Poles not only boycotted Jewish businesses, they smashed storefronts. Renia spent many evenings looking out her window, watching for anti-Jewish troublemakers who might burn down their house or harm her parents.

People responded to the antisemitism in different ways. Renia frequently heard her father speak of the need to move to a Jewish homeland where they wouldn't be bound by class or religion. Other Jews had different ideas. The largest party was the Bund, a working-class socialist group that promoted

Jewish culture. This group hoped that the Poles would realize that antisemitism wouldn't solve the country's problems. They insisted that Poland was the Jews' homeland, too, and they should stay exactly where they were and demand their rightful place. The Bund organized self-defense units, intent on staying put. They lived by the motto: "Where we live, that's our country."

As Renia grew up, she likely joined her older sister, Sarah, at youth group activities. Nine years older, Sarah was one of Renia's heroes. Sarah was intelligent—she liked to talk about grand ideas and principles—and she cared about doing good. The sisters wore the modern fashion of the day—berets, fitted blazers, and shin-length pleated skirts—and they kept their short, dark hair pulled back in neat clips. Jews were not allowed to join the Polish Scouts, so they joined various Jewish youth groups of their own. In Jędrzejów, young Jews had a thriving youth group scene.

There were several Zionist youth groups—some more intellectual, others more focused on charity—but all shared the values of heroism, courage, and honor. Sarah and Bela, Renia's older sisters, joined Freedom, a group of socialist Labor Zionists. Labor Zionists hoped for a homeland where they would live in collectives, speak Hebrew, and feel a sense of belonging. The groups offered activities such as readings, sports, and cultural events, and they celebrated working the land, believing that growing one's own food went hand in hand with communal and personal independence. For many of them, youth groups were like extended families, made up of friends, mentors, and boyfriends and girlfriends.

The Freedom group set up training camps and communal farms (*kibbutzim*) as preparation for immigration to Palestine. They taught manual labor and cooperative living. Renia was too young to join Freedom herself, but she likely spent her early teens tagging along with her older siblings, absorbing their passions, and taking it all in.

In 1938, fourteen-year-old Renia completed her basic education, and she was not able to continue with secondary school. (In some accounts, she claimed she had to quit school because of antisemitism; in others, because she needed to earn money.) Instead, she enrolled in a stenography course and trained to become a secretary.

In the summers, the youth groups organized summer camps. In August 1939, the young Labor Zionists attended programs where they danced and sang, studied and read, played sports, slept outdoors, and led discussions. They talked about ways to move to Palestine so they could carry out the work of their group's ideals. They wanted to save the world.

On September 1, 1939, the summer programs ended and the young people returned home to start school.

That same day, Hitler invaded Poland.

TWO

No Place to Run

September 1939

Renia heard the rumors. The Nazis had invaded Poland and were looting and burning down Jewish businesses and killing Jews at random. She wasn't sure how much of what she was hearing was true, but she did trust the news that the Germans were coming to Jędrzejów and they would be looking for Jews. Hitler was putting his program of violence into action.

No one knew where to go. Some Jews shuttered their houses and packed their bags. Trains were not running, so they walked in groups from town to town. Renia and her family joined their neighbors, heading east to Chmielnik, a similar small town on the other side of the Nida River, which they hoped was outside the German army's reach. The Kukiełka family had relatives in Chmielnik. They took nothing with them when they set off by foot.

On their twenty-one-mile journey, they walked through a battleground. They passed dead people and animals, killed by German bombings. Airplanes dropped explosives on all sides of them, sometimes close enough to knock Renia off her feet. A plane flew low and peppered the air with machine-gun fire. She heard the bullets whistle past. Mothers clutched their children to their bodies. Some babies cried; others were too silent, already dead. It was a day and night of hell to reach Chmielnik.

When they arrived, it was already too late. In Chmielnik, Renia and her family found the town a bombed-out disaster. People from Chmielnik had fled to Jędrzejów, hoping for safety there. Renia heard rumors that Nazis had taken over Jędrzejów. The first thing they did was round up ten Jewish men and shoot them in the town square. These murders were a warning to the local Jews, showing what would happen if anyone disobeyed them.

At that point, people believed that only the men were at risk, not women and children. Many Jewish males, including Renia's father, Moshe, hid in the countryside, thinking the crisis would pass quickly. The wealthy rented horses and fled to Russia. Houses stood empty.

In a matter of days, Renia saw German tanks approach

9

Chmielnik. Only one young Jewish boy confronted them. He ran out with a gun, shooting. Nazi bullets took him down. Within ten minutes, the Nazis were strolling through town, entering houses and restaurants, looting food, and taking what they wanted.

Renia peeped through a crack from the attic where she was hiding with her mother and siblings. She saw burning houses and doors shuttered, windows locked. Renia heard the non-stop pop of machine guns, buildings being demolished, moans and cries. Men and boys were taken outside to be shot in the courtyard. The town's wealthiest Jews were locked in the grand synagogue; the Nazis then burned the building to the ground.

She heard a knock at the iron gate in front of the house where they were hiding. The Germans smashed the windows and entered the house. Her family quietly pulled up the ladder to the attic. She froze and heard the Nazis going through the house. Then, silence. The Nazis had left. The Kukiełkas were safe. For now.

At nine the next morning, Renia stepped onto the street and looked around. About one quarter of the population was dead.

That was the first night.

For ten days, Renia and her family tried to make sense of what was happening. Thirsty Jews were forbidden to walk on the streets to search for water. Outside, the air smelled like rotting flesh. The Germans promised an end to the killing as long as people obeyed them. People went back to work, but many were starving. Bread was rationed, and the Jews were the last to receive their share.

Renia's father returned, and the family decided to walk back to Jędrzejów. They didn't have anywhere to go but home.

THREE

Zivia

December 1939

While Renia and her family settled into a new normal under German rule in Jędrzejów, the Jewish youth movement was growing stronger in other parts of Poland. Instead of disbanding when faced with Nazi threats, the young people redoubled their efforts, thanks to a handful of courageous young comrades. Many of these leaders could have fled to safety but chose not to.

One of them was Zivia Lubetkin, a serious girl. She was born in 1914 into a lower-middle-class and religious family in the small town of Byten, near the Russian border with Poland. Zivia attended Polish state elementary school, as well as Hebrew school. She was clever and had an excellent memory. Instead of attending high school, she worked in her father's grocery store. She was timid and shy; to boost her confidence, her parents made her stand on a kitchen chair and give speeches when guests came to the house.

Zivia was dedicated to the ideas promoted by the youth group Freedom. Despite her shyness, she moved to a kibbutz and began working on the land. Like many other group members, she wore baggy clothes and a leather jacket. The first time she returned home for a visit after moving to the kibbutz, her parents almost didn't recognize her.

On the kibbutz Zivia became vocal and unafraid to speak her truth. She was known for settling disputes and she earned the respect of those around her. With her strong beliefs and work ethic, Zivia was promoted to leadership roles. She became the national coordinator of training programs for The Pioneer, a union of several Zionist youth groups, and she and her boyfriend Shmuel, whom she'd met on the kibbutz, moved to Warsaw. In August 1939, she went to Switzerland as a delegate at the twenty-first Zionist Congress. She had a chance to flee Europe for the safety of Palestine, but she refused.

By the time Zivia set back to Poland, France had closed its borders. Roads were blocked, and trains had been rerouted. She made her way to Warsaw, the capital of Poland, on August 30, two days before Hitler invaded the country.

In the first days of war, Zivia and her comrades were told

to head east, to parts of Poland that were taken over by Russia instead of Germany, and where Jews still had relative freedom. By November 1939, dozens of branches of Freedom were active in the Soviet area, continuing to promote their Zionist socialist values.

Zivia worked on finding ways to get Jews to Palestine after passing through Romania. She sent her boyfriend, Shmuel, to test one of the escape routes, but he was caught and imprisoned, and she never heard from him again. Zivia was devastated, although she kept her feelings to herself.

In response to the loss of Shmuel, Zivia threw herself even more fiercely into her work. Another comrade, Frumka, who had already returned to Warsaw to lead the youth there, wrote to the heads of Freedom to request that her dear friend Zivia return, too, claiming that she'd be the best person to deal with the new Nazi government. The senior leadership had left Warsaw, and the movement needed experienced leaders.

Zivia agreed to return to Warsaw, heading straight toward danger. On her journey, secretly hiking through neck-deep snow, Zivia had to travel with a group of male Polish students who were trying to get home. The men had been courteous to Zivia while on Soviet land, but in Nazi territory, their attitude changed. Zivia became inferior. At the train station, she watched as several Germans slapped a group of Jews and told them they could not wait in the same waiting room as Poles and Aryans (Hitler's name for the Caucasian master race). The Polish students complained that Zivia should be thrown out too, but she stood firm. She had learned to stand her ground and hold her head high, even when people tried to degrade her.

Zivia had been gone from Warsaw for only four months, but she returned to a dramatically divided landscape. Antisemitic legislation had been put into place right after German occupation, and new discriminatory laws were passed almost daily. Jews were no longer allowed to work in factories owned by Christians or to take trains without special permission.

When Zivia glanced around at first, aside from a few bombed buildings, things looked much like they had before. The roads were filled with elegant cars, carriages, and red trams. Flowers lined balconies, and parks were lush.

But then there was the Jewish neighborhood. Zivia first visited one of the youth movement headquarters. The building was nothing but rubble. Next, she went to the Freedom headquarters. Zivia was stunned to find hundreds of young people who'd made it to Warsaw from small towns across Poland—the commune provided refuge for youth fleeing their hometowns. They in turn were shocked—and thrilled—to see her. The group threw a spontaneous party in her honor, claiming it was "an official holiday," serving extra rations of bread and jam.

When Zivia and Frumka found each other, they hugged and then began to review everything that had happened since the Nazis attacked, what had been done, and, most important, what to do next.

*   *   *

Both Frumka and Zivia were twenty-five, which made them among the oldest members of the group. Frumka Płotnicka had been born in the overwhelmingly Jewish city of Pinsk. She had a high forehead and straight hair and was the middle of three daughters in a poor, religious family. Frumka's father had trained to be a rabbi, but on his own rabbi's advice, he instead became a merchant to support his family. Frumka's parents could not afford to educate her, so she was taught by her older sister, Zlatka.

Frumka was a socialist Zionist who joined Freedom at age seventeen. She was fully committed, which was an extra sacrifice for a poor girl whose family would have needed her to work. Although she was a deeply analytical thinker, she was stiff and had a serious personality. She had trouble connecting with people and making close friends. But she worked very hard, caring for comrades and managing retreats. She was good in a crisis and proved herself ready to lead when needed.

Frumka could usually be found wrapped in her wool coat, in a corner of the room, listening. She remembered every detail she heard or saw. She was a trusted advisor and rose through the leadership ranks of the movement. Like Zivia, Frumka dreamed of moving to Palestine, but in the summer of 1939, she was given an assignment in the east. After Hitler's invasion that fall, instead of seeking safety, she requested that the Freedom leaders allow her to leave the area where her family lived and return to Nazi-occupied Warsaw.

First, Frumka returned to Warsaw.

Now Zivia was there, too.

Frumka and Zivia sat in a quiet corner at the headquarters, and Frumka told Zivia what she'd achieved over the past three months. She had led the group in establishing aid programs. Freedom was known for offering food, employment, and comfort in these times of hunger, confusion, and scattered families. Their focus had shifted from just sustaining their own members to helping the suffering Jewish masses. Zivia, who'd always championed social equality, was immediately on board.

With support from "the Joint"—the American Joint Distribution Committee, or JDC, founded to aid Jews across the world—Frumka established a public soup kitchen that fed six hundred Jews. She set up study groups and coordinated with other movements. Frumka realized they needed to establish long-distance connections to communicate with other groups so they could monitor the political situation and continue teaching their socialist ideals.

That first evening, as they ate bread and jam, Zivia and Frumka decided to try to find escape routes to Palestine, in addition to helping the community. To do both, they needed to hold fast to the movement's values: its celebration of community, and its pride in Jewish heritage.

* * *

Not long after she arrived, Zivia left the headquarters to make connections and to begin lobbying at the "Judenrat." From the beginning, the Nazis decided to pit Jew against Jew. The ghettos, they decided, would be managed and policed by Jews themselves, Nazi-controlled councils known as "Judenrats." These Judenrats registered all Jewish citizens, issued birth certificates and business permits, collected taxes, distributed ration cards, organized labor forces and social services, and ran their own Jewish police forces or militias. In Warsaw, these policemen wore caps and boots and were armed with rubber clubs. Some Jews claimed that they were forced into the Judenrat at the risk of being killed. Some hoped that by volunteering to participate, they would save their families or help save their communities. (It didn't work.)

Zivia wasn't afraid of the Warsaw ghetto Judenrat. She pestered them for additional food ration permits and refused to be intimidated. She sometimes spent entire days at the main Jewish community organizations, where she talked with the heads of welfare associations, exchanged information with other youth group leaders, traded underground publications, and convinced rich Jews to lend her money.

She also tried to protect young people from being taken to work camps. In Warsaw, all Jews aged twelve to sixty were subject to forced labor. When they needed workers, the Germans would block off a street and snatch all the Jews who happened to be there. People were herded into trucks and driven away to do hard labor while being beaten and starved.

Although the Jews experienced despair, hunger, and occasional violence, no one had any idea of the horrors that were yet to come. For now, these young Jews were social activists, passing on their values by teaching history and social theory. For now, they were busy strengthening the groups that would soon serve a very different purpose.

In the spring of 1940, Zivia arrived at the Freedom headquarters one day to find her friend Yitzhak Zuckerman, who was nicknamed Antek. He was tall, blond, and handsome, with a full mustache. He and Zivia had developed a close friendship back in the Soviet zone. Antek had returned to Nazi-occupied territory to join Zivia and Frumka as leaders.

Frumka maintained connections between Warsaw headquarters and the Polish towns, offering support and recruiting new members. She often traveled for work, and, some guessed, to avoid Antek and Zivia. She was romantically interested in Antek, but it was clear that he had feelings for Zivia, her best friend. Antek sometimes told the story of how he saw Zivia deliver an impassioned lecture, pounding her fist for emphasis, and recalled that as the moment that he fell in love.

In the evenings, Zivia, Frumka, and Antek led those at the headquarters in singing quietly and sharing stories of bravery in Jewish history. They read books, studied Hebrew, and debated the issues of the day. They held on to their beliefs about compassion and social action in a world of terror. They were preparing for a future they still believed in.

"Zivia" became the secret code name for the entire Labor Zionist movement in Poland.

FOUR

Terror in the Ghetto

April 1940

In Renia's hometown of Jędrzejów and across Poland, the Germans issued rules designed to single out, humiliate, and weaken the Jews. So Germans could tell the difference between Poles and Jews, all Jews older than ten were ordered to wear white armbands with Stars of David, which Zivia called "badges of shame." If someone removed the armband—or if it was dirty or the wrong size—the punishment was death.

Jews could not walk on the sidewalk. They had to take off their hats when they passed Nazis. Jews had their property stolen and handed over to Poles who had part-German heritage.

Jews became servants in their own homes or they were thrown out to become panhandlers on the streets. Jewish shops were taken over.

In April, a "Jewish neighborhood" was established. Renia's family was told that they had two days to move to an area a few blocks off the town's main square, which had previously housed the town's poorest residents. They could take only what they could carry, so they had to leave behind their furniture and all but a few small bags. Jewels were hidden or sewn into clothing, and people baked money into cookies. Some families gave their sewing machines, fine candlesticks, and other valuables to Polish neighbors, hoping they would someday get them back. Renia overheard some Poles walking through town, talking about what might become theirs next.

The crowding was impossible. Every apartment housed several families; as many as fifty people could be squeezed into a small dwelling. Renia slept on a sack of flour. Some families moved in with people they knew; most had to live with strangers.

In Poland, the Germans established more than four hundred ghettos, crowded areas where Jews were segregated. Ghettos were designed to concentrate the Jews so they could easily be captured and sent to camps, where they would be forced to work or face death. At first, Renia and her family were allowed to leave the ghetto in order to work and find food. Poles could enter the ghetto to sell or trade bread for valuables. But later, the gates were locked. Jews could only leave with a passage certificate issued by the Judenrat. Anyone who left the ghetto without permission could be executed.

Renia accepted the risk and snuck out of the ghetto to help her family. She and one of her sisters put on layer after layer of clothing—two pairs of stockings, dress on top of dress. They tucked extra shirts into their waistbands to make it look like they were pregnant, and stuffed small articles into their pockets, all available for sale. They waved a quick goodbye, and together they made their way down the street. Renia never revealed how they exited the ghetto: they may have bribed a guard, squeezed through a loose slat or grate, or climbed over a wall or across a roof. Because Jewish men were often kidnapped on the street for slave labor, they stayed home. It was easier for women to sneak out and sell whatever they had to offer.

The Kukiełka sisters made it to the village. They tried to draw little attention. Renia's heart pounded. Anyone who suspected they were Jewish could report them or have them shot. Anyone could pretend to buy something from Renia, then refuse to pay or threaten to turn her in to the Gestapo, the German secret police. Then what could she do?

Renia thought longingly of how she used to go with her mother to the bakery every Friday, picking out cookies, all colors and shapes. Now, this was her life.

Renia and her sister knocked on a door and a Polish woman answered, ready to bargain. The woman offered a small amount of coal for some heirloom lace placemats. Renia asked for a few coins, still far less than the goods were worth. They settled, and the girls headed back quickly. It wasn't much, but at least they had done something to help the family.

All Jews were supposed to work. Jews worked as tailors, seamstresses, and carpenters; others dismantled houses, repaired roads, and cleaned streets. People hid their injuries or weaknesses so they could keep working and get a bit of food.

Too often workers arrived home late, exhausted, covered in bruises, and disappointed that they couldn't provide more for their families. Some tried to sneak food into the ghetto, but the food was confiscated when they were searched at the gate. Many mothers had to leave their children to care for themselves, with older siblings keeping an eye on the babies and toddlers. Despite the beatings and terror, the Jews had no choice but to return to their jobs every day. Staying alive was itself a form of resistance.

One morning, a soldier knocked on the Kukiełkas' door. He said that two hundred and twenty strong, healthy men were to be taken to a forced labor camp outside of town. Aaron, one of Renia's younger brothers, was on the list.

The Kukiełkas begged Aaron not to go, but he feared that if he didn't his whole family would be punished, even killed. Renia's insides burned as she watched her brother leave, unsure if she would ever see him again.

Aaron was taken to a forced labor camp near Lvov. During the war, the Nazis set up more than forty thousand camps to murder what they called undesirable races. These facilities included labor camps, concentration camps, and extermination camps. The government leased some of the labor camps to private companies that paid them per slave worker. Women cost less than men, so companies often put females to work at "male" hard labor. At both state-owned and private labor camps across Poland, conditions were so bad that people died from starvation, beatings, illness, and exhaustion. Even though forced labor was better than being sent to an extermination camp, it was still a death sentence for many Jews.

Despite the country's social collapse, a limited postal service still functioned. One day, a letter arrived from Aaron. He was alive, but the horrors of his life shocked Renia: the boys slept in animal stables on straw that was never changed; they worked from dawn to dusk and were freezing and starving, eating wild berries and weeds picked from the ground to stay alive. They were beaten daily. At night, they were forced to exercise, and if they couldn't keep up, they were killed.

Like Aaron, so many Jews had been sent to the unknown. "A father, brother, sister or mother," Renia wrote. "Every family had one person missing."

As time passed, Renia came to understand that only "one person missing" was good.

Even "one person alive" meant you were lucky.

* * *

One night, the Kukiełkas received a notice that they, along with four hundred other families in the ghetto, were being forced to leave town—by midnight. The family packed their possessions onto a sled. They were taken to Wodzisław, another small Polish town. This was part of the German plan: moving Jews from town to town for no reason other than to shame and depress them.

When they arrived, the Jews were herded into a freezing synagogue with icicles hanging from the walls, and they were fed soup from a communal kitchen. Once the most affluent and influential people in their community, they now accepted that the only important thing was to stay alive.

"The result was that the Germans hardened the hearts of the Jews," Renia wrote. "Now each person cared only for themselves, willing to steal food out of the mouth of their brethren." As one survivor remarked, over time in the Warsaw ghetto people's souls became embittered: "If you saw a dead body on the street, you took its shoes."

In all the ghettos, the German decrees became harsher and more cruel.

"One day, the Germans invented a new way to kill Jews," Renia wrote. At night, a bus of German police would arrive with a list of thirty names. They would grab the men, women, and children from their beds, beat them, and then shoot them. In the night, Renia heard cries for help and mercy, as well as gunshots. In the morning, she saw the dead in the alleys and streets. She mourned for the lost and worried that one of her own family members might be next. Where did the list of names come from? Who did you need to fear? People were afraid to speak.

What could a fifteen-year-old do? Besides bartering for food, Renia tried to gather information. She heard rumors from other towns. People were starving. Thousands of Jews were forced to walk from the ghetto to the train station, and they were sent to unknown locations. Most disappeared. Where were they going?

Any Pole who helped a Jew would be killed. That was the law.

Jews in the ghetto feared that if they escaped, their entire families would be murdered in response.

Death had become commonplace. Nazis and their collaborators wore black uniforms and hats decorated with skulls. When they entered the ghetto, people scattered and hid.

"For them," Renia wrote, "killing a person was easier than smoking a cigarette."

FIVE

Education and the Word

October 1940

On Yom Kippur—the holiest day of the year in Judaism—the dining room at the Freedom headquarters in Warsaw was filled with young people who were captivated by a lecture about Jewish pride and the importance of social responsibility. The sermon accompanied a period of fasting and prayer that focused on atonement and repentance.

The speaker was Hantze Płotnicka, the little sister of Freedom leader Frumka Płotnicka. She was four years younger than Frumka and in many ways her opposite. While Frumka was darker in both coloring and disposition, Hantze was blond and bubbly, and she usually wore her hair in braids. Things always seemed to come easily to Hantze, from making friends to learning languages. Hantze had grown up leading the local kids, skipping and climbing trees, always at the head, laughing. The sisters were usually referred to as "Hantze and Frumka," with Hantze first, even though Hantze was younger. Her energy simply demanded attention when the sisters walked into a room.

When Hantze was fourteen she joined the Freedom group. She was incredibly smart and had sophisticated taste and a love of poetry. She became an active member and participated in seminars and events. When the Nazis invaded, Freedom sent Hantze to the east, to boost morale in the Russian-occupied area. But after several weeks Hanzte knew she needed to turn around and be with those who were suffering most. Her initial attempt to cross the border to the Nazi-dominated part of Poland failed when Hantze tried to swim across a cold river and had to turn back. She insisted on trying again.

Now, as Hantze addressed the Yom Kippur crowd, Frumka burst through the doors to announce that the Jewish Quarter was going to be sealed off. They were going to lose all ties to the outside world. The members had heard of this happening in more remote towns, but they didn't think it would happen in Warsaw, a European capital city.

When the ghetto was locked and more than four hundred thousand Jews were trapped in a tiny area surrounded by thick walls, Freedom workers rededicated themselves to providing aid, education, and cultural activity. They thought that Jewish pride and cultural enrichment was the only way the Jews would survive German occupation.

Freedom was not alone in this effort. Many organizations hosted cultural and aid activities. Ghetto Jews performed in shows and concerts. They staged satirical performances in coffeehouses and educational performances in theaters. There was a "Broadway" in the Warsaw ghetto consisting of thirty performance venues on one street alone. The Bund established seven soup kitchens and two tearooms, as well as a school system, day camps, sports organizations, an underground medical school, literary events, and a "Socialist Red Cross."

Education was a priority for Freedom. The group hosted three large seminars, despite Judenrat opposition. They offered religious classes, literary readings, and science lectures. Zivia worried about the ghetto children losing out on their education, so Freedom set up underground elementary and high schools, serving a hundred and twenty students. Thirteen teachers traveled from apartment to apartment, lecturing on Bible studies, biology, mathematics, world literature, Polish language, and psychology. They taught students who were shivering and bloated from starvation "how to think."

Freedom also offered training on caring for youngsters. The orphanages, once run by the Polish government, fell into disrepair. Many ghetto children—both orphans and those whose families had been taken away—lived on the streets, trading goods or begging for bread. Zivia, Antek, and other youth organized a "Children's kitchen" to feed the children and to teach them reading, writing, Hebrew, and Yiddish. "With all our strength we tried to give them back a bit of their sweet childhood, a bit of laughter and joking," one female comrade wrote.

The Freedom community, largely run by women, consisted of more than a thousand members. They spent hours singing with the children, taking them out for walks and to play in open areas. Older Jews would watch the children having fun, a spark of hope for the future.

Freedom needed books to enrich their spirits. Yiddish and Hebrew books, as well as titles by Jewish writers, had been banned and burned. Anti-Nazi publications were forbidden and anyone caught with them faced imprisonment or death. It was also illegal to keep a diary. Jews resisted by writing and saving their stories.

At considerable risk, Freedom started publishing its own books. Their first book, produced on a machine that printed one page at a time, was a collection of stories about Jewish suffering and heroism. They wanted to show young people clear examples of Jewish courage. Several hundred copies were printed and smuggled out to Freedom branches across the country. They also published educational handbooks and plays. When the press was in use, the children sang in their loudest voices to cover up the noise.

Underground newspapers offered information about the ghettos and camps. Freedom published one in Polish and Yiddish that discussed current events. Later, they put out a Yiddish weekly with news they received from their secret radio. Overall, among all the underground groups, some seventy publications were secretly printed in Polish, Hebrew, and Yiddish. Print runs were small, but each copy was read by multiple people.

Jews wrote their personal stories to maintain their humanity. Writing helped them find meaning in the senseless brutality that had become their world.

Conditions in the Warsaw ghetto deteriorated rapidly. Diseases spread. Jewish businesses closed and work was hard to come by. Desperate pleas for food were constant. Freedom continued its work inside and outside the city.

Zivia frequently left Warsaw to meet with local activists and set up lines of communication that could function across ghetto walls. She sent comrades from Warsaw to remote towns to share information. These messengers—usually young women with blond or light brown hair and blue or green eyes, women who looked traditionally German or Polish—taught the local chapters to create groups of five people who would work together to carry out their educational mission.

One of these early couriers was Chana Gelbard. For her first mission, Zivia gave her fake Polish documents and she pretended to be a traveling merchant, meandering between towns by wagon. Instead of selling goods, she distributed movement literature. She shared information about Freedom's activity, showing people in other locations that not everything had been destroyed. She encouraged her comrades to draw strength from their history. The youth listened breathlessly. At least for a moment, Chana's words helped other young Jews feel "strong against the clouds in these stormy times."

These girls—"Zivia's girls"—were becoming one of the most important parts of the resistance.

SIX

Becoming the Jewish Fighting Organization

December 1941

By the end of 1941, a network of youth resistance groups began to form across Poland. These groups shared information about what was happening in other parts of the country. A messenger came to talk to Zivia in Warsaw and told her about the atrocities happening in Vilna. She relayed this story: Sara, a young Jewish girl, had been taken to Ponary, a killing ground outside Vilna, where Jews were shot next to enormous pits. Sara was shot but not killed. She later woke up in the grave, surrounded by the dead. That night she climbed out and ran back to her hometown. Hysterical, she tried to tell people about what she had seen, but many people wouldn't believe her. It was simply too horrible. The leader of the Vilna youth movement, however, believed her and insisted that all Jews must be warned and fight back.

The messenger traveled from one ghetto to another, sharing this urgent message: The Nazis planned to kill *all* Jews.

It was time to resist.

How do you react to news that you are going to be killed? Do you try to stay optimistic to keep your sanity? Or do you fight back?

When Zivia heard about the mass execution, she didn't doubt it for a second. Other Jews had escaped from death camps and shared their own shocking stories.

If anything, Zivia felt guilty. Why hadn't she seen more clearly that the Nazis meant to kill all Jews? Why hadn't she done more sooner? Precious time had been wasted.

A number of courier girls, including Frumka, spread the news of the mass shooting and their understanding of Hitler's plans. Witnesses who escaped testified in front of large gatherings of community leaders, but they, too, were often not believed. Many Jewish communities simply couldn't accept these horrific stories; others didn't think it could happen in their part of the country. It seemed too barbaric to be real. In addition, they thought their communities were needed for labor, so it made no economic sense for the Nazis to kill them all.

In one account, a young Jewish woman tells of getting on a train to Auschwitz. Suddenly, she saw a note card being shoved between the wooden slats of the train. She read: "This train is taking you to the worst death camps. . . . Do not enter this train."

But the woman ignored this warning. It sounded too crazy to be true.

Zivia believed it was true. In her darkest moments, she considered suicide but she wanted her life to have a purpose: not to save lives, but to save honor, to not go quietly. She wanted to fight back.

A Polish underground had developed to fight the Nazis, but Freedom and the other youth movements had no contact with them at that time. They wanted help and support from community leaders and other adults, but the adults didn't listen. Instead, they criticized the youth leaders for "irresponsibly sowing the seeds of despair and confusion among the people."

Freedom members grew frustrated. Why wasn't anyone doing anything? Zivia and her comrades knew they had to work on their own. First, they needed to tell the Jews the truth about what was happening. Freedom knew how to publish underground bulletins, but they didn't know how to form an army or fight back.

Zivia kept pushing. In March 1942, she helped initiate a meeting of Jews from a variety of parties. The leaders of

Freedom pleaded with other groups to understand the urgency of preparing a Jewish defense movement. They got nowhere. Zivia worried that it was already too late.

In the summer of 1942, the Germans began mass deportations from the Warsaw ghetto. The Nazis would surround communities and gather hundreds or thousands of Jews, forcing them into trains for transport to death camps. It had started in April, on what became known as "Bloody Sabbath," when Germans invaded the ghetto at night and gathered and murdered Jewish intellectuals. From that point on, terror ruled.

There were constant stories of roundups and shootings. One day a poster appeared, declaring that anyone who did not work for the Germans would be deported. The deportations went on and on. The Jewish police had quotas for how many Jews they had to round up each day; if they didn't meet the numbers, their own families would be taken. After taking the young and old, those not working, and those named on various lists, the deportations were organized by street.

Jews were told they would receive three kilos of bread and one kilo of marmalade if they left voluntarily. Some people hoped it was for the best. Many, starving and desperate to remain with family members, took the offer. "That's how the life of a Jew became worth a slice of bread," wrote one underground leader.

The ghetto was emptying, the numbers growing smaller each day.

* * *

Fifty-two thousand Jews were deported from the Warsaw ghetto in the first mass deportation. Freedom comrades met with community leaders to discuss a response. They proposed to attack the Jewish police—who weren't armed—with clubs. They also wanted to incite mass demonstrations. But the young people were warned not to upset the Germans. The youth felt that the adults were being outrageous in their overcautiousness.

On July 28, Zivia and others in her youth group met and established their own defense force: the Jewish Fighting Organization. In Yiddish, it was *Yiddishe Kamf Organizacie*. In Hebrew, *EYAL*. In Polish, *Żydowska Organizacja Bojowa*. This group was no powerhouse. It had no money and only two pistols. What they had was a vision: to stage a Jewish protest.

The Jewish Fighting Organization was to be a countrywide operation, carried out by the connections that Zivia had already put in place. Now she would send her young female couriers out on life-risking missions, not to distribute educational material or share news, but to organize preparations for defense.

Zivia was the only elected woman leader of the Jewish Fighting Organization. She had a fake ID—her papers said she was a Christian and her name was Celina—but she had to stop traveling because she had dark hair and eyes, which led many people to assume she was Jewish. Instead, she became part of a fighting group. She learned to use a firearm and trained to be a guard. Many of the other female leaders, including Frumka, snuck out of the ghetto and tried to collect weapons.

The Jewish Fighting Organization decided to mark its territory. One night, the group went out into the silence of the ghetto after curfew on their first mission. They divided into three groups. One group posted billboards on buildings explaining that going to the camps meant certain death, so Jews should hide or defend themselves. "It is better to be shot in the ghetto than to die in Treblinka!" the signs read. Treblinka was a death camp.

The second group—Zivia's group—snuck outside the ghetto and set fire to abandoned homes and warehouses that were filled with goods stolen from Jews when they were sent to their deaths. The third group planned to execute the chief of the Jewish police. They wanted revenge, but they also wanted to spread fear among the Jewish police who were enforcing the Nazis' orders.

The groups met up at headquarters a few hours later. The signs had been posted, the fires set, and the police chief had been shot but not killed. The Jewish police had been afraid to attack the shooter, as they had hoped. Zivia was elated.

By late summer, the Jewish Fighting Organization had collected five guns and eight hand grenades. Frumka was the first to bring in weapons; she smuggled the guns by hiding them under potatoes in a large sack. Vladka Meed, a courier with the Bund's youth group, brought in dynamite.

The Jewish Fighting Organization debated whether to launch an offensive fight or just defend themselves. As they debated strategy and tried to obtain weapons over a three-month period, three hundred thousand additional Jews were taken from Warsaw to the gas chambers. At that point, 99 percent of the children from the Warsaw ghetto had been killed. Only about sixty thousand Jews were left within the ghetto walls.

On September 13, several dozen comrades gathered to discuss what to do. The mood was somber. "We came together and sat," Zivia wrote, "mourning and bleeding." They discussed group suicide. They considered taking whatever gasoline, kerosene, and guns they had left and setting fire to German warehouses, shooting a few Germans, and fighting to their deaths. Zivia was willing to die for the cause, and she believed it would be better to die resisting the Nazis than passively boarding a train to a death camp.

Antek, Zivia's boyfriend, disagreed. "The proposed act is an act of despair," he said. "It will die with no echo." Instead, he argued they should keep up the fight and begin collecting weapons again. He reminded them that their movement believed in the collective over the individual. They had to stay alive to resist.

So Zivia began to prepare for their next phase: gathering weapons to create a militia.

SEVEN

On the Run

August 1942

On a warm August morning in 1942, seventeen-year-old Renia woke from a nightmare and entered another. The morning sun soothed her, but only for a moment. As soon as she saw her parents, she knew that something was wrong. They told her about the horrors of the night: a nearby town had suffered a deportation, and the people who tried to escape had been shot.

"Your father and I are still young, but we've had joy in life," said Renia's mother, who was in her midforties. "But these poor babies, what wrong did they do? I would gladly die right here, right now, to spare the babies' lives." She desperately wanted to save her children.

In the past weeks, escapees from nearby villages had come to their ghetto in Wodzisław, where they'd heard Jews still lived. These runaways brought with them horrific stories of murder and cruelty. Renia did what she could to help, giving out clothes and food as she was able.

Renia met five young siblings whose mother had hid them in closets, under beds, and inside blankets when she realized that the Germans were rounding up Jews. Minutes later, a Nazi entered and began searching the room. He found them all.

But instead of killing them, he gave them each a slice of bread. "Hide still until nightfall," he said. He promised that their mother would return and escape with them. When the children expressed their gratitude, the man laughed, then began to cry. He said he was a father and his heart would not allow him to kill children.

Their mother never returned. At dawn, the eleven-year-old sister led her siblings out through the window, looking for neighbors. They left town, eventually making their way to Wodzisław, where families took them in. Still the children asked, "Where is Mother?"

Renia felt the situation was deteriorating with every minute. Every day she survived was pure luck. No one slept at night, which was probably best, since that was when the Nazis usually attacked. Everyone was trying to leave. But where was it safe?

Did any towns still have Jews? They had no weapons, nothing.

A large number of ghetto Jews escaped one night, running to the forests and the fields. Those with money bribed the townspeople to hide them in attics, cellars, and sheds. Some Jews wandered with no destination. In the end, most were killed.

Renia had an advantage over many other Jews: she had green eyes and light brown hair, which made her look like she could be Polish. Many people who did not have strong Jewish features tried to "pass" as Christian and start their lives over. Those with money and connections bought fake travel documents and moved to new cities where no one knew them.

It was easier for girls, who got jobs in offices or stores and as actresses and housemaids. Some joined nunneries. It was harder for men: if the Germans suspected that a man was Jewish, they ordered him to pull down his pants to see if he had been circumcised. (Circumcision is a procedure involving the removal of the foreskin of the penis; it is a Jewish religious practice called a bris.) If a man had been circumcised, he was presumed to be Jewish.

Even for those "imposters," life was difficult. They were often blackmailed or turned in to the authorities for a reward, such as a kilo of sugar or a bottle of whiskey. Some children were sent to orphanages as Christians; others worked selling newspapers, cigarettes, and shoe polish.

Renia and her family knew they had no choice but to leave.

They had heard rumors that a deportation would take place any day. They gathered all the cash they had and divided it equally among the children. They decided to split up: Renia's parents and her little brother would go into the forest. Her two sisters would travel to Warsaw and hide with relatives until their parents could join them.

The goodbye was heartbreaking. Renia could barely stand her father's tears, her mother's wails, and their final hugs before parting. But Renia had to go, and she had to go alone.

"No matter what happens," Renia's father told his children, "promise me you will always stay Jewish."

On Saturday, August 22, Renia joined her brother Aaron at a Nazi-run Jewish labor camp in a small town. A while earlier, Aaron had escaped from the first work camp and pretended to be a Pole wandering the woods. He was moved to another camp where he built train tracks. The guards liked him, so he had arranged for Renia to join him. About five hundred Jewish boys paid to get jobs at the camp, believing they were safe from deportation as long as they were working. There were also twenty Jewish women who did light labor, like counting bricks.

Renia arrived at the camp with a friend from the ghetto. She worked doing light labor. Renia tried to convince her supervisor to allow her father and sisters to come to the camp, but it was too late. The commander told her that the girls were no longer going to be allowed to work at the camp, and he would have to send her away on the next deportation. She was not safe.

"Escape," he whispered to Renia. "Go wherever you can."

Renia didn't want to run again. Where would she go? Who would go with her?

"You are still young," the German said. "Run away, and maybe you will make it out alive."

On August 27, Aaron helped Renia and her friend reach the forest, near where he worked. He then said goodbye, unsure if he would see her again.

The girls began to wander through the trees. Suddenly they heard screaming, gunshots, dogs barking.

The girls ran, chased by two policemen. When they were caught, they were taken to a small building for train conductors that held other Jews who had been caught. When the police began to question her, Renia said in perfect Polish, "Do you really think I'm a Jew?"

"No," he said. "You look and speak Polish. You are one of us. Walk away, quickly."

The girls left together. Renia worried that her friend did not look Polish. Would she bring unwelcome attention?

Then Renia heard shots. Her friend was on the ground in front of her. The police had shot her in the back.

Renia walked off quickly, burying her anguish.

Renia was on her own.

For days Renia wandered through the forest, trying to stay alive. She finally reached a small village and boarded a train heading for a town where she knew a railway worker who had been friends with her parents. When she reached her destination, she got off the train and saw a woman's purse on the ground. She grabbed it and took some money and even more useful—a passport. These papers were Renia's ticket to safety—she could use them to pretend she wasn't Jewish.

She hurried over to the home where her friend lived. She was exhausted, hungry, and desperately wanted a shower and clean clothes. When he opened the door, she was shocked to see a warm, orderly, and comfortable home—a sight from another life. He and his wife were pleased to see her but concerned. They fed her tomato soup with noodles and gave her clean clothes and underwear.

As they were talking, they heard their young son through the open window. He told their neighbor that a girl named Rivchu (which was Renia's nickname) was visiting.

"That's a strange name," the neighbor said.

"Well," the boy said, "she's a Jew."

Renia's hosts bolted from their seats and pushed her into a cupboard, covering her with clothes. Renia could hear the knock on the door.

"No, no, no," her hosts said. "We had a guest, not a Jew."

That night, her friend handed Renia money and a train ticket. She was off again, searching for a place where she could feel safe.

This time she had clean clothes and a new name, Wanda Widuchovska. It's not clear if this was the name on the ID she'd found on the street or if she had received new identification papers from a priest who was trying to help. Renia's friends had used a marker to blur the original fingerprint and put her own on top. Jews used several types of fake documents, including identity cards, birth certificates, travel permits, work cards, and baptismal certificates to show that they were not Jewish. The best type of fake ID was a real one, from a deceased or even a living person. As Renia understood, having the right identification was an issue of life and death.

Renia boarded a train for Kazimierza Wielka (Kajee-MEER-ja Vee-EL-ka), a village where she'd heard Jews still lived. She looked up and saw a man staring at her. He was from her hometown, and he recognized her.

She overheard people talking. "Yes, this is her," said a voice in the darkness. "She has it easy. She doesn't resemble a Jew."

Renia didn't know what to do. She froze and her vision went blurry. She thought she would faint as she looked around and saw people who she was sure wanted to capture her. She got up and moved to a little platform at the end of the train. The car door opened, and the conductor appeared. "Good evening," he said.

She knew he was testing her accent, to see if she was a Jew.

"It's so cold out," he said. "Why don't you come inside?"

"Thank you for your kindness," Renia said. "But the cars are so crowded and stuffy. I'd rather get some air."

He looked at her ticket, checked her destination, and went back inside.

She knew that he was going to hand her to the authorities at the next station.

The train slowed down as it began to go up a hill. It was now or never. Renia threw her tiny suitcase off the train, then jumped after it.

For several minutes, she lay unconscious by the side of the tracks, then the cold jolted her awake. Her legs hurt, but she was alive.

She made her way to a small house in the distance. A dog barked, and the landlord approached. "What do you want?" he asked.

"I'm on the way to see my relatives," Renia said. "I don't have a certificate proving my Polish origin, and I know the Nazis are searching. I need to wait out the night somewhere safe. If Germans see me during the day, they'll know right away I'm not a Jew." Renia's ID was not valid in this area, so she made up excuses.

The man brought her inside and gave her a warm drink. He showed her to a bushel of hay where she could sleep. "You must leave in the morning," he said. "I'm not allowed to accept guests without registering them." At least she had a few hours to rest, to plan.

The next morning, Renia set off again by foot, eventually reaching Kazimierza Wielka. The Jews of the town remained alive but tense, knowing that the nearby villages had already been wiped out. Even the best-hearted Christians were not helping Jews hide at this point, fearing for their lives.

The Nazis had declared that no one could take in Jewish refugees. The Jews obeyed, hoping they could avoid deportation and death. Renia felt relieved to see the Star of David armbands, reassured that other Jews still lived. One evening, she confided to a Jewish policeman that she was Jewish. "Where can I spend the night?" she asked.

He warned her not to wander through the streets. He let her stay in the corridor of his house until morning. He and his family were the only people who knew she was Jewish.

At the time, Poland was divided into three parts: a part annexed by Germany in the west, a part annexed by the Soviets in the east, and in the middle the General Government, a German zone of occupation established after the Nazi invasion. Kazimierza Wielka, where Renia stayed, was in the General Government. Renia got a job as a Polish housekeeper in the home of a half-German family. She disguised herself as a simple, happy-go-lucky girl, never letting her employer know her heartache. Her boss adored her and never registered her with the police.

To convince her boss that she was a Christian, Renia said that she wanted to go to church but she did not have the right clothes. The family that hired her gave her church clothes.

Renia had grown up around Polish children at school, but she had never been to Mass. She didn't know Catholic rituals, hymns, or prayers. She went to church, fearful that she would be recognized as a fraud. She watched those around her and imitated every motion.

When the service was over, she was relieved. Her employers and neighbors had witnessed her performance. She passed.

Renia had written a letter to her sister Sarah, who lived at a Freedom kibbutz in Będzin (BID-jean). Even in 1942, the postal service still functioned, and the letter made it through. A few days later, a letter came back!

The letter said that Renia's parents and siblings were still alive. They were destitute, but they had found shelter in the forest. Aaron remained at the labor camp. Sarah had been able to maintain communication with her family.

Renia lived day by day, hour by hour, waiting, worrying. Her family warned that it was too dangerous for her to stay where she was without the proper documents—the one she had found was not good for this part of the country. Renia knew that if her employer eventually decided to register her with the police, she would be exposed.

It was time to move again. Renia decided to join Sarah on the Freedom kibbutz in Będzin.

EIGHT

Heart of Stone

October 1942

Renia needed help reaching her sister. Sarah arranged for a Polish woman to help Renia travel to Będzin. On a cool autumn evening, Renia served the family she worked for their dinner, then she approached her boss. "My aunt fell ill," Renia said. "They called for me to come quickly, to care for her for a few days."

Her employer understood. Why wouldn't she trust her best employee?

Renia's heart beat wildly as the train pulled out of the station. She knew that the train would be passing Miechów, the town where her parents and younger brother were living. She longed to see them and was determined to stop on the way.

The train arrived at a small station. "Is this Miechów?" Renia asked.

"Not yet," her smuggler said. "Soon, soon."

Later, Renia asked again. "This one?"

"We cannot get off at Miechów."

"What? Why?" Renia asked.

"It will make your journey too difficult," the woman whispered. "I don't have time to take you."

Renia pleaded.

"I promise," the woman said, "that as soon as I get you to Będzin, I will turn back and go to Miechów. I will get your parents and your brother. I will bring them to you in Będzin."

"No." Renia put her foot down. "I must go see them now."

"Listen," the smuggler said, leaning into her. "Sarah said you absolutely cannot go to Miechów. I cannot take you there."

Renia considered leaving the train alone, but she trusted her sister, who was older and wiser.

When the trained stopped at the Miechów station, Renia remained glued to her seat, her heart leaden, her brain a fog.

En route, Renia spent a few days at the smuggler's house in Częstochowa. During that time, Renia thought about Sarah. It had been several years since she'd seen her sister, and she worried that they might not recognize each other.

They resumed their travel and crossed the border from the General Government to the area of Poland that had been annexed by the Third Reich without incident. Once Renia arrived in Będzin—where there was no closed ghetto— she walked through the town to the Freedom kibbutz. She bounded up the stairs and found a room with young men and women, all dressed in clean clothes, sitting around tables, reading. Where was Sarah?

A young man, Baruch, introduced himself. He knew who Renia was. He led her up two more flights of stairs to the sleeping quarters. The room was quiet, dark. She heard the muffled sound of moaning. It was Sarah, in bed.

"Sarah," Baruch said. "Would you like it if Renia came to see you?"

Sarah jumped out of bed. "Renia!" she cried. "I was sick worrying for you."

Sarah's kisses and embraces were warm on Renia's skin. Despite Sarah's weakness, she led Renia to the kitchen to feed her. In the light, Renia could see how skinny her sister's face had become, all bone and edge. She looked older than her twenty-seven years, but Renia was overjoyed to see her.

The sisters tried to come up with a plan to save their parents. The smuggler's promise to bring them over had been a lie. There was not enough room for the Kukiełkas in the kibbutz, and besides, Sarah didn't have enough money to pay the smuggling fees.

Renia received a letter from her parents. They were in Sandomierz, living like animals in tiny, moldy rooms, where they slept on the ground or on a thin mattress of hay. They had no food and no fuel for heating. They spent their days worrying about deportation and death.

Her youngest brother, Yankeleh, wrote a letter begging for help. He longed to be with his sisters. He worried about their parents and did his best to help them hold on to hope. He escaped from the ghetto each day and tried to make a tiny bit of money.

Renia felt sick. What could she do?

They received another letter, a final farewell. "If we don't survive, then please fight for your lives," her parents wrote. "So you can bear witness. So you can recount how your loved ones, your people, were murdered by sheer evil. May God save you. We are about to die, knowing that you are going to stay alive . . . This is our fate. If this is God's will, we must accept it."

The letter also told of the fate of Renia's two sisters, Esther and Bela, who had been sent to a death camp.

Renia shed no tears. "My heart," she later wrote, "turned to stone."

She assumed her parents and most of her siblings were dead. She had to remind herself that now she lived for her sister Sarah and her Freedom comrades. This was her new family.

Renia and Sarah stopped getting letters from their brother Aaron. They learned that he had been transferred to a factory where Jews were forced to do brutal labor. They heard that he had contracted typhus, an infectious and deadly disease spread by lice. His health was fragile.

Still, Renia and Sarah were alive—and determined to fight.

NINE

A New Way Forward

October 1942

Renia was not alone in her drive to resist. Chajka Klinger was a twenty-five-year-old Jew eager to prove herself on her first mission with the youth movement. She tucked her curly short brown hair behind her ears, and looked around carefully as she passed through the streets and alleyways of Będzin distributing flyers that revealed the truth about what was going on. Chajka knew the risk, but she felt relieved to finally be *doing* something.

Chajka had been born in 1917 to a poor religious family in Będzin. She was clever and passionate, and she received a rare scholarship to attend a top-tier Jewish prep school, where she became fluent in several languages. Będzin was an early host of many Zionist movements and the hub of twelve youth groups. Chajka became a member of The Young Guard, which blended support for a Jewish homeland with Marxism. It appealed to her intensity and passion; she believed The Young Guard movement would eventually lead the Jewish nation to a complete social and national revolution. Chajka was drawn to the group's philosophy, and her boyfriend David was a dedicated member. Chajka and David, a slim boy whose pockets were stuffed with newspaper articles, met at the library when they both wanted to take out the same book. The librarian let David have it since he was their number-one reader. Chajka was upset and pretended not to know him. But months later, he submitted a poem to the journal that she edited, and she was taken by his passionate writing. Chajka quickly became a regional movement leader. She was extroverted, sensitive, and always falling in love.

In the late 1930s, the couple joined a kibbutz. They were supposed to move to Palestine in September 1939. When the Nazis attacked Poland, Chajka and David tried to escape the country, but they couldn't get out. They were ordered by The Young Guard headquarters to stay in Będzin and salvage the movement.

The Jews in their area were forced to work in German factories. Dozens of textile factories produced clothing, uniforms, and shoes for Nazi troops. Jews worked for meager salaries and bits of food, but conditions were much better than at labor camps. Several factory owners protected their workers from deportation. One notable example was Alfred Rossner, a German who never joined the Nazis and tried to save thousands of Jews from being sent to death camps.

Chajka and David oversaw underground work and community aid. She began with the poorest children, finding them shoes and clothes, cleaning them, and feeding them what she could. Będzin's Freedom kibbutz became a social center for all the youth movements. Frumka Płotnicka frequently traveled the two hundred miles from Warsaw to run seminars. Freedom organized Hebrew classes, a library, and children's programs. Sarah, Renia's sister, cared for the children and helped run the kibbutz's orphanage.

In the first winter of occupation, the group organized a Purim festival. Traditionally, Purim is a joyous holiday during which Jews dress in costumes and perform comedy skits. Dozens of children sang and laughed and enjoyed the festivities. Chajka couldn't believe how many people had shown up, even during a war.

By the fall of 1942, Będzin's youth movement was in its prime, and Chajka was right at the center.

One night, the Germans came to take the Jews to labor camps. Chajka waited in the night as soldiers forced their way onto her street, into her building, inside her apartment.

The military men ordered Chajka to dress and go with them. Her mother cried and begged the Nazis to leave her daughter alone. Chajka urged her mother to be quiet. "Don't you dare beg them or humiliate yourself in front of them," she said, remaining calm.

At least two thousand girls from town were rounded up and taken to a municipal school building. She found four friends, comrades—Leah, Nacia, Dora, and Hela. The Będzin girls were pressed together tightly, their faces nearly touching. An ocean of heads crying, screaming, laughing.

The room was stuffy. Leah, one of Chajka's Young Guard coleaders, pushed her way from one room to the next, opening windows for air. She collected the children and combed their hair, comforting them and giving out bread. "Don't cry," Leah said. "They are not worth your tears."

In the morning, the classification began. Each woman presented the German commissioner with her work certificate. Those who worked at the weapons factory—including Leah—were freed.

But she didn't run. Leah waited near the school for other girls who were coming out and took their work papers. She passed the papers back into the building to give to other girls who didn't have valid documents. This scheme saved a large number of girls who were released as workers rather than sent to camps.

The Germans fell short for their quota for deportation, so they captured women off the street. Leah didn't have her papers any longer because she had passed them to another girl. She was deported to a labor camp.

Leah wrote letters to Chajka from the camp, telling of

hunger and beatings, even for women. Half the day, she worked in the kitchen, half in the sick ward. She snuck bread to prisoners and tried to influence the other women to act with justice and compassion.

This wasn't the only deportation. The Nazis returned in May 1942 and again in August.

The Jews of Będzin were told to report to the soccer stadium the next day for a document check. At first, the youth movements warned the Jews not to attend. They suspected it was a setup. After some debate, they changed their minds and decided to go.

At 5:30 a.m., thousands of Jews walked to the stadium, dressed in festive clothing, as instructed. They sat on bleachers, waiting, thirsty in the hot sun. They were suddenly surrounded by soldiers with machine guns. At three p.m., it began to pour with rain and "the selection" started. People were divided into three lines—those going home, those going to labor camps, or those going to the death camps.

Families were torn apart. As people began to realize what the three lines meant, chaos erupted. Eight thousand to ten thousand Jews were locked into buildings guarded by soldiers.

The youth leaders of Będzin did not quietly go along with the plan. They knew that thousands of Jews outnumbered the police and guards. They decided to act. They gathered the children who were going to be deported, and at their signal, the children broke into a sprint and ran. Some youth stole police hats and, posing as police, pushed people into the safe lines. They smuggled Jews out in giant soup pots. They created chaos.

The Jews destined to be killed were held captive in the orphanage building until the train arrived to take them to the death camp. The women of the youth movement convinced the Judenrat that they needed to set up an infirmary inside. The nurses comforted and bandaged the sick, but they also helped as many women as possible escape by taking off and distributing their uniforms. Jewish women left the building dressed as nurses, then smuggled the uniform back into the building so another woman could escape also pretending to be a nurse.

One of Chajka's friends discovered a pathway from the attic through a block of unguarded civilian houses to the outside. The women busted a hole in the wall and snuck Jews out through this passage, too. Every person who escaped was a small victory.

During this time, Będzin's youth movements, including The Young Guard and Freedom, began working together. In the summer of 1942, Chajka invited Mordechai Anilevitz, a Young Guard leader from Warsaw, to speak. Chajka held Anilevitz in the highest esteem, calling him the "pride of the movement" as a brave and practical leader. Members from various Zionist groups assembled in the Będzin youth kitchen to listen to a two-hour speech given by Anilevitz called "A Farewell to Life."

In his remarks, Anilevitz told them about the gas chambers and death camps. He also told them about resistance efforts that were underway in Vilna, Białystok (Bee-AL-ee-stock), and Warsaw. He called for action, and, if necessary, honorable deaths.

Another branch of Warsaw's Jewish Fighting Organization was officially founded that night in Będzin. It included about two hundred comrades from various youth movements. Będzin had already established a strong connection to Warsaw, and couriers shared information. The groups also sent secret-coded postcards from Będzin to Switzerland, asking for help and telling of the activities of the Jewish Fighting Organization in Warsaw.

Chajka was transformed by Anilevitz's call for self-defense. She became one of the Jewish Fighting Organization's fiercest supporters. She believed that armed defense—to fight as Jews, alongside Jews, defending a Jewish legacy—was the only way forward. Chajka wanted to share the truth of what was happening so the movement would grow and the resistance would become more powerful.

It wasn't easy to form a military corps. Like the group in Warsaw, the Będzin branch of the Jewish Fighting Organization also lacked weapons, training, money, and contact with Polish underground groups. Anilevitz had to return to Warsaw, leaving the Będzin branch of the Jewish Fighting Organization without a leader. Finally, in late September, Zvi Brandes arrived as a resistance leader. He was respected for his strength and rock-like build, as well as his organizational skills.

Zvi organized comrades into groups of fives, as the youth had done in their education model. Not only were these five-member groups fighting units, they also published bulletins, letters, and a daily newspaper. This is when Chajka began distributing underground flyers, telling people the truth, telling them that the time had come to rebel.

Despite the wartime chaos, Renia felt at peace in Będzin. Many comrades worked during the day, then labored in the kibbutz in the evenings. Renia was assigned to work in the laundry.

When Hantze Płotnicka arrived on the kibbutz, she brought more positive spirit. Hantze knew all the kibbutz members and noted their unique strengths. Hantze had been staying at a farm outside Warsaw, but she was sent to Będzin when the farm was shut down. Renia was impressed by how Hantze gathered the members for philosophical discussions after a hard day of physical labor. She maintained connections with groups in other towns, as well as her sister Frumka, who was still in Warsaw working with Freedom.

Hantze told the group about the terrible conditions at the farm. When comrades began to complain about the difficulties in their lives, Hantze would tease them. "In Grochov, the conditions were much worse," Hantze said. "And even they stayed alive . . ."

* * *

The comrades on the kibbutz continued to hear news that confirmed their worst fears. They learned details about what was happening at Treblinka, a death camp northeast of Warsaw where Jews were systematically murdered and cremated. Frumka arrived and shared horror stories of what was happening across Poland, of Jews being killed by the thousands. "There's no help coming from anywhere," Frumka said. "The world has forsaken us." After telling what she knew, Frumka asked for one thing from each member: that they fight back using whatever means they could find!

These stories energized the Jewish Fighting Organization. They dreamed of buying guns. They established their first workshop, where members made knives and experimented with homemade explosives. Chajka could not wait to set one off!

The spirit of rebellion was in the air. That autumn, the nearby town of Lubliniec was the site of an unplanned revolt. One afternoon, Nazis ordered all the Jews to gather in the market and undress. Men, women, and children were forced to remove their clothing, even their underwear. They were told the clothes were needed for the German army.

Nazis stood over them with whips and sticks to force them to comply. Suddenly, a dozen naked Jewish women spontaneously attacked the officers, scratching, biting, and throwing stones at the German soldiers. They weren't going to take it anymore.

The Nazis panicked, shocked and outnumbered. They dropped the clothing and ran.

TEN

Fighting Back

October 1942

It was right around this time that young Jews organized the first armed revolt, in Kraków, the capital of the General Government, and one place where the youth movement continued to flourish. Gusta Davidson was one of its leaders.

One fall morning, Gusta arrived in Kraków exhausted but thrilled to be back with her fellow Jews. The ghetto had been formed more than a year earlier, but it was constantly changing. Jews fled, then refugees came from other villages, as if it were a safe haven. It seemed that everyone moved from one city to the next, running in circles until they ran out of money or strength—or they fell into Nazi hands.

When Gusta looked around, she sensed that many of her fellow Jews had almost lost the will to live. The youth, on the other hand, had such a lust for life that they pushed themselves toward resistance even if it meant certain death.

When she entered the ghetto, she was met by several comrades who took care of her. From the time she was introduced to Akiva, a local Zionist youth group, Gusta was drawn to the ideals of self-sacrifice and loyalty. Unlike some of the other Zionist groups, Akiva emphasized Jewish tradition. Every Friday night, they celebrated the Sabbath at an Oneg Shabbat ceremony. When they became members, people swore to uphold a pledge.

Just months before, the Akiva youth group had been based on a peaceful farm in a nearby village. Gusta's husband, Shimshon Draenger, also an Akiva leader, called a meeting to warn that the war was going to be worse than they'd imagined. Like their comrades in Warsaw and Będzin, they realized that the movement had to change its approach. "We want to survive as a generation of avengers," Shimshon said at the meeting. "If we survive it has got to be as a group, and with weapons in our hands."

Gusta knew both she and her husband were at risk of arrest. The couple made a pact that if one of them was caught, the other would surrender, too.

They accepted the need for violence and revenge. By August, they merged with The Young Guard, Freedom, and other groups to form Kraków's "Fighting Pioneers."

I pledge to engage in active resistance within the framework of the Jewish Fighting Organization of the Chalutz Youth Movement.

I swear by everything most dear to me, and above all by the memory and honor of dying Polish Jewry, that I will fight with all the weapons available to me until the last moment of my life to resist the Germans, the National Socialists, and those in league with them, the mighty enemies of the Jewish people and of all humanity.

I pledge to avenge the innocent deaths of millions of children, mothers, fathers, and aged Jewish people, to uphold Jewish spirit, and to raise the flag of freedom proudly. I pledge to shed my own blood fighting to achieve a bright and independent future for the Jewish nation.

I pledge to fight for justice, freedom, and the right of all human beings to live in dignity. I will fight side by side with those who share my desire for a free and equitable social order. I will serve humanity faithfully, dedicating myself without hesitation to achieving human rights for all, subordinating my personal desires and ambitions to that noble cause.

I pledge to accept as a brother anyone willing to join me in this struggle against the enemy. I pledge to set the seal of death on anyone who betrays our shared ideals. I pledge to hold out to the end, not to retreat in the face of overwhelming adversity or even death.

Gusta had pledged herself to these ideals, and she intended to live up to them.

The Nazis made Kraków the capital of the General Government in place of Warsaw, so the city was heavily protected. A number of high-ranking military officers lived and worked in the area.

Gusta knew that her husband, Shimshon, was planning some kind of momentous battle. She was safer not knowing any details. Secrecy remained critical. The teams of five each had their own weapons, provisions, operating area, and an independent plan of action. Only members in a group knew who the other members were and knew of its plans. If someone was captured, they could not reveal details of the broader plan.

Shimshon was also in charge of counterfeiting documents. He was an amateur typesetter and had experience etching and engraving. He carried his equipment—his "floating office"—in a briefcase before Gusta set up an apartment for them in a small town outside Kraków. Their home was a beautiful villa with a large room with two windows and a kitchen. She placed flowers on the table, curtains on the windows, and pictures on the wall—all to give the space a homey feel, like a cozy nest. Gusta's six-year-old nephew Witek was with her, and Shimshon played the role of a hardworking father. People thought he held a government job. No one suspected that they were Jewish or that their apartment housed the Jewish resistance's forgery factory!

In the evenings, after Shimshon arrived home, Gusta covered the windows, locked and bolted the door, and the couple worked until three a.m., forging documents and writing and publishing their weekly underground newspaper *The Fighting Pioneer*. Gusta and Shimshon made two hundred and fifty copies that were distributed throughout the Kraków region.

Hela Schüpper was an active member of Akiva and the underground. She had a fair complexion and full, rosy cheeks, and Hela used her charm and sophistication, as well as the savvy she gleaned in her studies at business school, to disguise herself as a well-to-do woman on her way to the theater. With her easy elegance, Hela had become the group's main courier, and she had made several trips carrying information and documents between Kraków and Warsaw. When she arrived in Kraków in the fall of 1942, Hela carried something different: a stash of weapons—five guns and several clips of cartridges. This was the start of a new era of defense for Akiva in Kraków.

The youth raised money to buy weapons and fake documents. Gusta and her female comrades searched the forests for potential bases and hunted for safe houses and hiding places.

Gusta grew frustrated that women were not included in

high-level resistance meetings. The group had many active, leading females, but they weren't trusted to make decisions. Gusta worried that the men could be hot-headed and stubborn. She hoped that the men would remember: every life counted.

On a warm October day, the Nazis began a deportation in the Kraków ghetto. Many Akiva members and their families lived in the ghetto, and they barely made it out; many were unable to save their parents. Gusta was shocked by the silence. In other towns, these mass deportations were loud and bloody affairs; here in the "capital city" it was quiet and orderly, with most of the Jews too weak from hunger to even scream or cry out.

The youth responded with action. They decided to target high-ranking Nazis living in town. They quickly set up bases inside and outside the ghetto, as well as contact points and safe apartments in surrounding cities. Small groups would confront their enemies, killing traitors and collaborators. When they encountered a target, fighters would jump from a dark alley, deliver a blow, confiscate a weapon, and disappear.

In Kraków, a first-floor, two-room apartment—13 Jozefinska Street—became the home and base for the youth resisters. Most of the comrades were the last living members of their families. They shared all they had. The group ate their meals together. Seven people slept on each bed; others rested on chairs or the floor. This was their last home, their last family, the last place where they could live their true identity as Jews.

The group kept up the tradition of observing the Sabbath. On Friday, November 20, they met for festivities from dusk to dawn. They'd spent two days preparing the meal, and they came together in white blouses and shirts, at a table set with a white tablecloth. They sang and prayed. Someone called out, "This is the last supper." The group sensed that their situation was about to change.

The fighters would soon have to leave the ghetto because of deteriorating conditions. One night, the leaders hid in a park and shot a Nazi sergeant as he walked by. No one caught them, and the youth succeeded in several more Nazi killings.

On December 22, when many Nazis were in town shopping for Christmas gifts and attending parties, forty Jewish men and women fighters headed into the Kraków streets. At seven p.m., they attacked three German coffeehouses. They bombed a Nazi Christmas party. Fighters threw grenades into a café where high-ranking Nazis gathered. They killed at least seven Nazis and wounded many more. They made a statement.

A few weeks after the December attacks, Hela was on a train when she struck up a conversation with a young Polish professor. "The war will soon be over," he said.

"How do you know?" she asked.

He explained that Polish forces had started to move. He was so proud that the Polish underground had blown up the cafés!

Hela needed him to know the truth. "You ought to be aware,

kind sir," she said, "that the attack to which you referred, on the Kraków cafés, was the work of young Jewish fighters. If you live to see the end of the war, please tell the world about it. And by the way, I, too, am a Jew."

The man was stunned. The train approached Kraków.

"Come with me," he said when they arrived. He could have turned her in. Instead, he brought her to a warm apartment to safely spend the night.

ELEVEN

Rebellion

January 1943

Zivia awoke startled at six a.m. The Nazis were invading the Warsaw ghetto. The Jews didn't expect them, not that day. But the Germans had received a new order, and they had new quotas to meet.

Zivia dressed and tried to figure out what was going on. A German soldier was posted in front of every house. There was no way to get out and no way to contact the other units. What could she do now?

Over the past months, the Jewish Fighting Organization in Warsaw had made steady progress. The youth groups had worked well together and collaborated with other military groups, including the Polish underground, which offered them a few weapons. By that point, they had obtained ten shotguns and they knew how to make explosives.

Members were dispatched across Poland to lead resistance units. In early December 1942, comrade Vladka Meed was approached by the underground and asked to leave the ghetto to do undercover work on the outside. She was told to exit the ghetto gates with a work brigade, and to bring with her the latest underground bulletin, which included a detailed map of Treblinka, the death camp. She hid the pages in her shoe.

At the gate, a Nazi inspector pulled her out of line and took her to a private room. He told her to undress. She left her shoes on. "Now the shoes!" he ordered. Just then, another officer rushed in and said that a Jew had escaped, and both of the men rushed off. Vladka quickly dressed and slipped out, telling the guard at the door that she had passed inspection. She managed to leave the ghetto and gave the hidden papers to their intended targets.

As part of their effort, the Jewish Fighting Organization wanted to attack certain heads of the Judenrat and Jewish police as well as other Jewish collaborators who they felt made the Nazis' job easier. They hung posters in the ghetto explaining that the group would avenge any crime committed against the Jews. To make the point clear, they killed two men who had been working with the Nazis. The Jews in the ghetto began to sense the power of the Jewish Fighting Organization.

Now the Jewish Fighting Organization in Warsaw was planning a full-scale uprising. After months of preparation, a date was set: January 22, 1943.

So that morning at six, Zivia was shocked when the Nazis began their major deportation on January 18, four days before the planned attack. The comrades weren't prepared and had no time to come up with a response. Most of the groups of five had no access to arms except for sticks, knives, and iron bars. The groups couldn't connect or coordinate their efforts.

There was no time to lose. Two units went straight into action. The first unit of Young Guard fighters entered the streets and let themselves be caught so they could be moved with other Jews. When unit leader Mordechai Anilevitz gave a command, the fighters whipped out their concealed weapons and opened fire on Germans who were marching nearby. Some of the Jews were able to escape.

The Germans were stunned. "The Jews are firing at us!" The Jewish youth kept shooting.

The Nazis regained their composure and came back with superior firepower. They chased down the few who had managed to run. Only two of the youth survived, but they had proved their point: Jews could kill Germans.

Zivia was in the second group, commanded by three men, one of whom was Antek. They took a different approach. Since most Jews were hiding, the Germans had to enter buildings to find them. This group waited for the Nazis to approach and planned to shoot at them from inside the building.

At an apartment building on Zamenhofa Street, forty fighters took up positions. They had four hand grenades and four shotguns between them. Most of them were armed with iron pipes, sticks, and light bulbs filled with sulfuric acid.

Zivia and her comrades expected to die in battle, but they expected to die with honor.

In the moments before the attack, there was silence. Sharp boots beat against the stairs. The front door flung open, and a gang of Germans burst in.

One comrade pretended to be reading a book. The Germans brushed past him, heading for Zivia's room. The man who was reading jumped up and shot two Germans in the back. The fighters burst out of closets and hiding places and began to fight with whatever weapons they had. They stripped the dead soldiers of rifles, pistols, and grenades.

The Germans who survived ran away.

The Jews had slayed the Nazis! And now they had more weapons.

Zivia felt confused. She had expected to die. She knew the Nazis would be back. The fighters hid an injured comrade, then climbed onto the snowy roof of the five-story building and found their way to another hiding place.

In time, the Germans tracked them down. Again, the Freedom comrades opened fire. Two fighters tossed a German down a stairwell shaft. Another threw a hand grenade, causing an explosion that blocked an entrance. The Germans did not return that night.

The next day, however, the Nazis came back.

Surprisingly, the comrades survived once more, with only one injury. That night, Zivia's group returned to a Freedom gathering place. They found the furniture broken and the feather pillows torn apart. The comrades who had been there at the time had been taken to Treblinka.

Holding back their sadness, the group settled in and waited.

At dawn, the ghetto was still. The Nazis sent the Jewish police to investigate first. They were scared that the Jews would attack again.

Zivia felt reinvigorated, like she had a new reason to live. That night she and her surviving comrades sat by a fire and rested. Then a lookout warned that there were German soldiers in the courtyard.

The Nazis entered the building, and the youth opened fire.

The surviving Germans retreated.

Again, Zivia was amazed that she and her comrades were alive. The fighters collected the dead soldiers' weapons and left through the attic.

When the Germans returned, they were already gone.

The January deportation lasted four days. In the end, the Jewish Fighting Organization ran out of ammunition, and many comrades died. Thousands of Jews were taken, but the effort was a success.

The Nazis did not clear the ghetto. They captured only half their quota.

The Jews had almost no food, but they had new hope. The resistance brought unity, respect, and status. It was a critical victory for the Jews.

There was hope in Warsaw but despair in Będzin. The winter was harsh. People became sick, and there were no medications. Each day, truckloads of Jews over age forty—considered too old or weak to work—were sent away. Jews were killed for breaking minor rules: crossing the street diagonally, walking on the wrong side of the sidewalk, breaking curfew, or smoking a cigarette. It was illegal to own eggs, onion, garlic, meat, dairy, or baked goods. Police entered Jewish homes to inspect what they were cooking.

Some of the comrades were growing weaker. Hantze became ill, and she was tortured by nightmares. Renia also began to feel the effects of hunger—fatigue, confusion, and a constant obsession with food.

The youth in Będzin were beginning to question their sense of purpose. Why bother anymore?

Then the rumors began. The Jews were told they would be "resettled" to a closed ghetto on the other side of the train station. At least twenty-five thousand Jews were to be held in housing meant for ten thousand. Should Freedom move to the ghetto or run?

After a heated discussion, they decided to move.

The Jews were shoved into the ghetto. Those who couldn't afford apartments were forced to build huts in the square, like chicken coops, for protection from the rain. Stables, attics, and even outhouses became homes. Ten people lived in a converted cowshed. Many slept with no roof at all. Renia said that Jews moved around like shadows or living corpses.

The ghetto was guarded by the Jewish militia. Anyone on the streets after eight p.m. was shot.

Every week, Renia watched as people were sent to Auschwitz to die. The youth, the old, Jews who hid their children, young people accused of being politically active, those who missed a couple of days of work—they were all taken away. The ghetto was becoming less crowded as residents were being taken each day, someone from every household. "All the hearts are broken," Renia wrote. "It's a wonder people maintain their sanity."

In February 1943, Renia attended a meeting of the Freedom leadership in Będzin. Frumka sat at one end of the table, Hershel Springer, another youth leader, was at the other.

"We've obtained a few passports," said Hershel.

Everyone gasped. These papers were like golden tickets out of Poland. Each passport offered a chance of survival. People with these documents were held in special camps and occasionally exchanged for German prisoners of war. It had taken months to get these documents, a hugely expensive and dangerous process that involved sending secretly coded letters with photos to special counterfeiters. Who would have the chance to escape?

A decision had to be made.

"Frumka," Hershel said, staring into her dark eyes.

She looked back at him, silent.

Hershel explained that the orders had come from Zivia in Warsaw. Frumka was to use the passport to leave Poland and go as a delegate to the UN's International Court of Justice in The Hague and serve as an official witness of Nazi atrocities.

"Leave?" Frumka asked.

Renia looked at Frumka. She could almost see her friend's sharp mind at work. Frumka was their leader, the rock supporting them all. What would they do without her?

"No," Frumka said. "If we must die, let us all die together. But"—she paused—"let us strive for a heroic death."

Everyone sighed. Frumka placed her fist on the table, firm as a gavel. "It's time," she said. "It's time to get energized."

And with those words, they knew what they had to do: keep on fighting.

PART TWO

Devils or Goddesses

"*They were not human, perhaps devils or goddesses. Calm. As nimble as circus performers. They often fired simultaneously with pistols in both hands. Fierce in combat, right to the end. Approaching them was dangerous. One captured [woman] looked timid. Completely resigned. And then suddenly, when a group of our men got within a few steps of her, she pulls a hand grenade out from under her skirt or her breeches and slaughters the [soldiers] while showering them with curses to the tenth generation—your hair stands on end! We suffered losses in those situations and so I gave orders not to take girls prisoner, not to let them get too close, but to finish them off with submachine guns from a distance.*"

—Nazi commander Jürgen Stroop

TWELVE

"I'll Go"

February 1943

The youth movement in Będzin was buzzing. After the call to go down fighting, the comrades worked from morning until eight p.m. curfew, preparing for what would come next. Those who had military experience taught others to fight, using firearms, flammable liquids, axes, hammers, scythes, grenades, even bare fists. They were trained to fight to the end, never to be taken alive. Renia and the comrades collected sharp tools, flashlights, knives—anything that could be used in battle.

The comrades were awed by weapons. Chajka carefully picked up a gun, hesitant. At first, she worried that it would go off accidentally, then she developed confidence. With a pistol in her hand, she felt like a real revolutionary.

The Polish underground and the Jewish Fighting Organization helped smuggle weapons into the ghetto. They developed workshops where comrades made brass knuckles and daggers, in addition to creating bombs, grenades, and bottles filled with explosive materials. As their skills grew, their homemade bombs became better than the ones they bought.

After working hard all day, the comrades spent the nights building bunkers. Couriers from Warsaw brought plans for the construction of elaborate hideaways and underground passages several kilometers long, opening outside the ghetto. The shelters were to be equipped with lighting, water, radios, food, and stashes of ammunition and explosives. The entrances were carved out in ovens, walls, closets, sofas, chimneys, and attics. Hiding places were set up in staircases, stables, and firewood storehouses. When the time came, all they would have to do was enter their well-stocked bunkers. They would be ready.

The Jews began to stand up to Nazi authority. In February 1943, the Nazis were preparing for another deportation and they needed more men in the Jewish militia. These men would be the ones to force their fellow Jews onto the trains. For the effort, the militia demanded that six male Freedom comrades join their forces. If they refused to comply, they would be deported to a camp in Germany.

The comrades refused. When they didn't show up at the assigned time, the Jewish police went to the kibbutz and took their work papers, even though they knew that if the comrades were caught without papers they'd be sent to forced labor or death. The next day, the Jewish police surrounded the kibbutz armed with clubs and orders to take the six defiant comrades to Germany.

Two of the wanted comrades jumped out a window and ran. The deputy commander ordered the police to take the remaining men hostage until the escapees turned themselves in.

Frumka worried that someone was going to get killed in the scrimmage, or worse, the Germans would arrive and kill everybody. She ordered those on the list to go to the police office, and the entire kibbutz followed them. Instead of surrendering, the situation turned into a brawl between the militia and the kibbutz. The ghetto residents watched and applauded.

Renia felt proud of this act of defiance, but Frumka feared that the Germans would hear of this and strike back with more force. She went to the militia commander and urged him to keep silent. He respected her and agreed not to report the runaways on the condition that they take hostages in exchange for the two escapees. Six comrades surrendered—three who were on the initial list, plus Hershel Springer, his brother Yoel, and Frumka, who had volunteered herself.

The higher commander learned about the conflict and ordered that the kibbutz be locked. Frumka and Hershel returned later, but they reported that because they humiliated the militia and its commander, all the men would be sent to Germany. They returned to the Judenrat to plead for the men. Late that night, they all returned. No one was sent away, drafted to the police, or put in forced labor.

The ghetto gossiped about Freedom's bravery. They were learning that it was possible to say no.

In February, Zivia wrote to Frumka, again demanding that she travel abroad. She needed to stay alive so she could tell the world about the "barbarian butchering of the Jews." She needed her to survive to bear witness.

For the same reason, in March Zivia sent a letter to Hantze, ordering her to go to Warsaw to be smuggled out of the country. "No excuse, no argument." This was an order.

Both Frumka and Hantze refused. This time, however, Frumka begged Hantze to go, and not wanting to disappoint her sister, she finally agreed. She put on peasant clothes, but Renia worried that she still looked Jewish with her facial features.

Two days later, Renia received a telegram reporting that Hantze had arrived in Warsaw. But then a few days later, she got a letter saying that her departure from Poland was delayed, and she would remain in Warsaw. Another letter reported that the general deportation might occur at any moment. "If you don't hear from us again, it means the [deportation] has begun," the note said. "But this time, it will be much more difficult. The Germans are not prepared for what we have in store."

A few weeks later, a courier told the Będzin group that there had been a terrible slaughter in Warsaw. A telegram reported that Zivia was dead.

Then, total silence from Warsaw. Nothing. No telegrams, no letters, no messengers. No information. No news. Was every single person dead? Had they all been murdered?

Someone had to go to Warsaw to find out what was happening. The group needed a courier who didn't look Jewish: Renia.

Renia didn't think about the girls who went missing, the disappearances, the deaths. She was a woman of action, with clear goals. She felt her anger, her rage, her need for justice.

"Of course," Renia said. "I'll go."

Renia's new world as a courier was filled with disguises. To be a Jew and live outside the ghetto was a constant performance, a life-or-death acting job that required intellect, intuition, and an animal instinct for danger. Renia knew that while it was hard to get out of the ghetto, it was much harder to be on the other side.

The same day Renia agreed to her new assignment, the Będzin Jewish Fighting Organization contacted a smuggler who knew the best way to travel to Warsaw. Renia set off from the kibbutz as she often had, with one exception: she had sewn money into her clothes, cash that might be useful to the Warsaw fighters.

Renia used the ID that she had found on the street months earlier. She and the smuggler took the train toward Warsaw, getting off the train one station before the border between the Third Reich Annex and the General Government.

Renia and the smuggler walked seven and a half miles through fields and forests to a small border crossing where the smuggler knew the guard. Suddenly, they were stopped by a soldier. The smuggler handed over a flask filled with whiskey. The soldier let them pass.

They tried to move in silence. Along the way, Renia heard a rustle in the leaves. Something—somebody—was close by. Renia and the smuggler fell to the ground and crawled beneath a bush. They heard footsteps approaching.

As the person approached, they could see that it was someone coming from the other side of the border. When they each realized that the other meant no harm, the man spoke. "From here, it's quiet," he said.

On the streets of Warsaw, Renia took in the sights. The city was not as she had imagined. The grand squares were clouded with smoke and ash. The air smelled bitter, like burning hair. There were police checkpoints at almost every intersection.

Renia had memorized every detail of the new ID provided by the smuggler. It belonged to his sister, but it had no photo or fingerprints. Nazi checkpoints followed one after another; Renia worried that the fake documents that worked in the countryside may not pass in the city.

"Papers," a police officer said. Renia handed over the ID and looked him in the eyes. He rummaged through her purse, then let her pass and board a trolley. Renia got off at her stop and walked alone toward the address she had been given.

Renia pulled herself together, then moved swiftly toward her target.

When she arrived at the address, she knocked. "I'm here to see Zosia," Renia said to the landlady. This was the code name of Irena Adamowicz, a Catholic woman who worked with both the Jewish and the Polish undergrounds.

"She's not here," the woman said.

"I'll wait for her."

"You have to leave," the landlady said. "Guests are not permitted. We can be killed for letting in a stranger."

Renia didn't know what to do. Where should she go? She knew no one in Warsaw. She wasn't sure she could pass those checkpoints again.

"Besides," the landlady said quietly. "I think Zosia might be a Jew." She paused, then whispered, "The neighbors are suspicious."

"Oh no, I don't think so," Renia said. Her voice was calm. "I once met her on a train and she told me to stop by if I was ever in town. She looks Catholic, not like a Jew."

Renia felt like the landlady could see all her secrets. Still, she kept on. "If she was a Jew," Renia said, "we'd sense it right away."

The woman nodded at Renia, pleased with her answer. Then she became still. Renia turned around.

There stood Zosia.

As she entered the apartment, the truth hit Renia: she wasn't just a Jew in disguise, she was an underground operative. She was a courier—*kasharit* in Hebrew—a word meaning "connector." Couriers were usually young women, aged fifteen to early twenties, who had been dedicated to their youth movements. They were energetic, skilled, brave, and willing to risk their lives.

Couriers played different roles as the war progressed. The courier practice began at the start of the war when women traveled between ghettos, connecting with comrades to teach, lead seminars, and share publications. These women formed networks to smuggle food and medical supplies. Travel was not easy, and it was considered suspicious to look lost in a new city.

The couriers were lifelines, "human radios," trusted contacts, and sources of inspiration. Thanks to them, news spread across the country. In addition to good news, they also brought reports of mass killings and deportations.

As the youth movements turned into militias, the couriers began smuggling fake IDs, money, information, underground publications, and Jews themselves. They found safe rooms for meetings, helped obtain work papers, and made men in the movement seem less threatening (by acting as if they were just a nice couple out on a stroll). Most women spoke better Polish than their male comrades, so they often bought their train tickets and rented apartments.

It was also less suspicious for women to travel during the day. They could carry handbags, purses, and baskets (for smuggling contraband) without looking suspicious. While Polish men were expected to be at work, women could go out on the street shopping without being immediately stopped or snatched for forced labor. Nazi culture was sexist, and women were not expected to be secret agents.

Most of the couriers did not look traditionally Jewish; they had light hair and blue, green, or gray eyes. They wore Polish clothes, often in middle- and upper-class styles. They also had to appear Polish in manners and mannerisms. Couriers needed to speak flawless Polish. Renia and many other couriers went to public schools and had Polish friends growing up, so they learned to speak without the characteristic Jewish accent.

Specialists in Warsaw helped disguise Jews. They taught the women how to style their hair and makeup. Bangs, curls, and frizz were all suspicious, so Jewish women learned to straighten their hair and sweep it up off their foreheads. They practiced cooking pork and ordering moonshine. They recited Catholic prayers, memorized the Lord's Prayer, and celebrated their friends' patron saints' days. Jewish expressions (like "what street are you from?") had to be replaced with their Polish counterparts ("what district are you from?"). The nuances were endless.

Couriers tended to have strong intuition. They were good at reading people and sensing their motivations. Couriers had fake IDs, fake personal histories, fake hair, and fake names. They also had fake smiles. Courier girls were trained to laugh. They had to pretend they had no cares in the world, even if their parents and siblings had been murdered, they were starving, and they were carrying bullets hidden in their jam jar.

"We couldn't cry for real, ache for real, or connect with our feelings for real," one courier later wrote. "We were actors in a play that had no intermission, even for a moment, a stage performance with no stages. Nonstop actresses."

The work was exhausting and terrifying, but that did not stop them from going out, day after day, night after night. Each girl followed the women who went before them. And in this spirit of selflessness and rebellion, Renia accepted her mission.

THIRTEEN

Inside the Gestapo

May 1943

Renia had heard stories about the couriers who came before her. She hoped that she could be as successful and daring as her Freedom comrade Bela Hazan. Bela was beautiful, and fearless.

Bela's father had died when she was six, and her mother raised six children on her own, living in a room in the basement under a synagogue in a Jewish town in southeast Poland. Bela's mother was uneducated, but she insisted that her children attend a Hebrew school. She was proud and washed their clothes each night so they'd look as neat as the rich children.

Bela's mother was a religious Zionist who allowed her to

attend movement activities, just not on the Sabbath. In 1939, Bela was selected by local leadership to participate in a self-defense course in preparation for life in Palestine. There Bela learned to use weapons, and she attended lectures by comrades, including Frumka and Zivia. She was chosen to be a defense instructor at the Freedom kibbutz in Będzin.

Bela was doing defense training when Hitler invaded. Some comrades were moved deeper into Poland, but Bela was told to stay and care for the Będzin kibbutz. The German attack was so violent that Bela and the others fled, although they returned several days later. The Freedom leadership asked her to go to Vilna, a journey that proved to be very challenging. She stopped to see her mother briefly, promising that she would reach Palestine and bring her over. It was the last time Bela saw her.

In Vilna, which was first under Lithuanian, then Soviet control, Bela joined in the thriving youth movement scene. The German invasion of 1941, however, brought horror. Anti-Jewish laws were put in place, but Bela remained strong.

Bela would leave the ghetto, then she'd tear off her Jewish Star of David patch, which she pinned to her clothes instead of sewing it (a criminal offense). She would go to the market to buy food and medicine for her friends. Because of her Aryan features, she didn't worry about being identified as a Jew by sight, but her Polish accent was very Jewish. At night, she returned to the ghetto, where she lived in a three-room apartment with thirteen families. At age eighteen, she found a job in a hospital as a nurse in the operating room.

Freedom leaders looked for non-Jewish-looking girls to work as couriers between the ghettos. Bela volunteered. She needed papers to be able to move freely. She approached a non-Jewish acquaintance at the hospital, telling her she wanted to go see her family. Bela's colleague lent her her own passport, and Bela Hazan became Bronisława Limanowska, or Bronia for short.

As a courier, Bela smuggled news, bulletins, money, and weapons between the Polish towns of Vilna, Grodno, and Białystok. She left the ghetto and bought a cross to wear around her neck as well as a Christian prayer book. When she reached Grodno, she knocked on a Polish woman's door. Bela told her that her house had been bombed, her family killed, and she needed shelter. The woman agreed to let her in.

In the morning, Bela went to the employment office.

"Can you speak German?" the clerk asked.

"Sure," Bela said. Yiddish was close.

The clerk quizzed her. "You speak very well," he said. Her bad Yiddish had come out as decent German. "I have a job for you," he offered. "You can be a translator—at the Gestapo office."

A job with the Gestapo, the official secret police of Nazi Germany?

The next day, she began working at the Grodno Gestapo, a mainly administrative office. The boss liked her immediately. Bela was in charge of translating Polish, Russian, and Ukrainian into German. She also cleaned and served tea.

A week into her job, Bela asked her boss for official papers stating that she worked for the Gestapo. He signed on the spot. With these, she went to the Grodno city hall, explained that all forms of her ID had been destroyed, and asked for a full new set of papers. The clerk was so afraid to mess with a Gestapo worker that he rushed her to the front of the line. They drew up an ID with false details.

Even with her new treasured papers, it was nearly impossible to obtain train travel permits. One morning, Bela went to work in tears. She told her boss that her brother had died in Vilna and she needed to bury him. (According to Polish tradition, he had to be buried in three days.) Her Gestapo boss went with her to get the train passes.

When she arrived in Vilna, she took stock of the situation, planning for the right moment to enter the ghetto and pin on her Star of David, which she kept tucked away in her wallet. Near the ghetto gate, a woman with long blond braids approached her. "Don't we know each other?"

Bela didn't recognize her. Who was this? "What's your name?" she asked, her heart racing.

"Christina Kosovska."

The woman took out a photo from her wallet. It was a group of comrades. Bela was among them! "My real name," she whispered, "is Lonka Kozibrodska."

Lonka! Bela remembered that she was a master courier who

was fluent in Polish and seven other languages. Poised and worldly, Lonka was in her late twenties, university educated, and from a cultured family outside Warsaw. She wore her long braids like a halo on her head. Comrades sometimes wondered if she had been sent by the Gestapo as a spy, but Bela trusted her right away. The two women blended into a workers group and entered the ghetto together.

At resistance headquarters, Bela delivered her fake ID to the Jewish fighters who were making false papers so they could copy it. After a few days, Bela returned to Grodno. She changed identities, switching her Jewish armband with a black ribbon of mourning. When she returned to work, she found a sympathy card from her Nazi office mates saying how saddened they were by the loss of her brother. This, at last, made her laugh. The Nazis mourned the loss of her make-believe sibling, but not the lives of the thousands of real Jews who were being killed every single day.

Just before Christmas 1941, Bela told her landlady that a friend would visit for the holidays. Tema Schneiderman—another courier known for her generosity and savvy—stayed with Bela for a few days. A Nazi who had a crush on Bela invited her to the office Christmas party, and she couldn't refuse. That night, Tema and Lonka were both staying in her apartment, so she brought them along. The three of them got dressed up and went to the party, at one point posing for a photograph. Each one got a copy.

Soon after, the underground called Bela to Vilna. She told her boss she needed to be in the hospital for two weeks. She took a train packed with Nazi soldiers; they had no idea she had a Jewish star in her coat pocket.

In the ghetto, Bela was relieved to be among friends and open as a Jew, even if she knew it couldn't last. She spent the next few months traveling from city to city, smuggling information, papers, and people. She finally stopped by her family home and found a Ukrainian family living there. Bela asked what happened to the local Jews.

"Gone," she was told.

Bela ran, then burst into sobs. Living for revenge was her only option.

In the spring, Lonka was sent on a mission to Warsaw. She was carrying four revolvers. And then she disappeared.

Bela volunteered to find out what happened to her friend. Bela's boyfriend, who she planned to marry after the war, gave her two guns. She hid them in her pockets. She also had a Hebrew underground bulletin printed on thin paper, which she wove inside her thick braids.

She passed all inspections with her fake papers. And then an officer boarded the train and approached her.

"Come with me," he said. "We've been waiting for you for a long time."

Without a word, Bela got up and followed him out.

The train left.

The police took her to a small room in the station. They searched her and found the weapons. There was nothing she could do but act as if nothing unusual was occurring. Men came to escort her to the forest, yelling at her to run. She didn't want them to shoot her from behind.

They arrived at a small prison in the middle of nowhere. Bela panicked: Would they find the Hebrew material on her? They knew she was an arms smuggler, but they did not know she was a Jew. She asked to use the bathroom, where she pulled the bulletin from her braids and threw it down the hole.

In a small room, everything was taken from her. The interrogation began. She lied about everything, and they beat her without mercy.

One of them asked, "Do you know Christina Kosovska?"

Lonka?! "No," Bela said.

"Tell the truth or I'll kill you." This time he took out the photograph of Lonka, Tema, and Bela taken at the Gestapo Christmas party. "Do you recognize yourself?"

Bela admitted that she knew Lonka, saying she met her for the first time at that Christmas party. They didn't believe her and beat her again, breaking a tooth.

After six hours of questioning, Bela was thrown on the cold dirt floor. The following morning, she was brought to Warsaw's Gestapo headquarters. Bela was put into another tiny room, and noted a German slogan on the wall: "Look only forward, you can never look back." Bela was tortured all night, then moved to Pawiak, a political prison in the ghetto.

Bela felt relief: she knew that Lonka was there.

Now that she was in Warsaw, Renia tried to learn everything she could so she could share information with comrades back in Będzin. After saying hello to Irena Adamowicz—the undercover Catholic Polish woman also known as "Zosia"—the two women went out into the city. As they walked around, Renia begged for information.

"Is it true that Zivia was murdered?" Renia asked.

It had been several days since Irena had contact with the ghetto. She said that as far as she knew, the reports to Będzin had been false. "Zivia is alive," she said. "At this very moment, she's fighting in the ghetto."

Renia exhaled deeply. This, she decided, she needed to see for herself.

FOURTEEN

The Warsaw Ghetto Uprising

April 1943

A few weeks earlier in Warsaw, the night before Passover on April 18, 1943, Zivia and her friends stayed up into the night making plans for the future. At about two a.m., a comrade announced that he had just received a warning. "The ghetto is surrounded," he said. "The Germans will begin their attack at six a.m." They didn't realize that it was Hitler's birthday, and a Nazi commander wanted to destroy the ghetto as a gift.

The Jewish Fighting Organization had been preparing for months, but it was hard to face the beginning of the end. Zivia and the others did not expect to survive.

Ever since the January "mini uprising," the attitude of the Jews in the ghetto had shifted. They no longer believed in the safety of work; they all realized that they were going to be killed—it was just a matter of when. Some Jews with money had escaped. Some built hideouts and tried to buy guns. The Jewish Fighting Organization was no longer a bunch of kids with homemade weapons, but a respected national struggle.

They began to get more outside help. The Polish resistance sent fifty pistols, fifty hand grenades, and several pounds of explosives into the ghetto. The Jewish Fighting Organization bought weapons from Poles, ghetto Jews, and German soldiers; they also stole them from the Polish and German police.

The youth developed a "munitions factory," where they made bombs out of water pipes taken from empty houses. They fabricated Molotov cocktails, gasoline bombs that could be thrown at the enemy to start fires. To raise money to buy weapons, they collected funds from every source they could find.

The leadership studied the ghetto streets and came up with military strategies. They wanted to surprise the Nazis, attacking chosen locations and then withdrawing through attics and rooftops. They had five hundred fighters—ages twenty to twenty-five—divided into twenty-two fighting groups. About one out of three were women.

The Jewish fighters trained, taking first aid classes and learning to strip and assemble their guns in seconds. Each group had a commander, a specific fighting post, knowledge about their particular area, and plans in place in case they lost connection with central command.

Zivia knew that the Warsaw ghetto fighters would not survive, but she did not want them to be forgotten. She wanted to keep their story alive. That's why she had written to Frumka and Hantze, asking them to leave Poland, and tell the world how the Jews fought back. Now, it was time to fight.

Despite the planning, it was still a surprise when the moment of conflict arrived. As the Jewish Fighting Organization messengers ran through the ghetto spreading the news, people took up arms or went into hiding.

Zivia was one of thirty fighters posted on the highest floors of a building near the ghetto entrance. As the sun rose, Zivia saw the German forces—two thousand soldiers, tanks, and machine guns—advancing toward them.

The Jewish Fighting Organization let the Germans pass the main entrance. Then . . . BOOM! The mines they had planted under the main street went off. Success!

When the next group of Nazis marched in, Zivia and her comrades threw hand grenades and bombs from the rooftop. As explosives rained from the skies, the Germans scattered, and the Jewish fighters chased them down with guns.

Zivia's unit fought for hours. Remarkably, *none* of the Jewish fighters was injured!

But that was just the first wave of fighting. They headed to find bread and a place to rest, but they heard a whistle, then the sound of motors. They ran back to their positions and again threw Molotov cocktails and grenades at the Nazi tanks.

The following days of fighting were difficult. Most bunkers lost electricity, water, and gas. Almost all the militia units were cut off from each other. The Germans fired on the ghetto nonstop.

Zivia made night tours of the fighters' posts and bunkers. One night she met up with comrades from other units. The bunker had been prepared as the medical unit, with a doctor, nurses, equipment, first aid, medicine, and hot water. Zivia heard their stories of success.

A woman fighter, Masha Futermilch, told stories of lighting and throwing bombs at the Germans. From below she heard them scream: "Look, a woman! A woman fighter!" Masha was awestruck. A sense of relief washed over her: she had done her part.

The Warsaw Ghetto uprising began days before Hantze was supposed to leave the city. Once fighting began, it was decided that rather than going abroad, Hantze should return to Będzin and help with defense. If she had to die in battle, she wanted to die alongside her sister and comrades there.

On the second day of the Warsaw uprising, during a break in the fighting, Hantze snuck out of the ghetto and began walking toward the train station, accompanied by two armed comrades.

"Halt!" a soldier called.

One of the armed comrades opened fire. The police fired back.

Hantze was killed.

After five days of fighting, the Jewish Fighting Organization was shocked to find that most of them were still alive. They had been prepared to die in combat, so they had not planned escape routes or made survival plans. It was not long before they grew tired, hungry, and weak. Zivia and her comrades now wondered, how could they keep going?

Renia stayed at a hotel outside the ghetto. As the ghetto burned, a contact of Zosia's took Renia to see for herself what was happening.

Every street bordering the ghetto was filled with German soldiers. The clouds were red, reflecting the flames of burning houses. The ghetto was completely surrounded, with armored tanks firing from all sides. Above them, German planes swooped low and hurled bombs, setting the streets on fire.

But Renia also saw Nazi tanks being destroyed by Jews.

Through the smoke, she could make out young Jewish men with machine guns firing from the roofs. She saw Jewish women shooting pistols and throwing explosives. Jews who were not part of any organization grabbed what they could find and fought back. There was no choice: the alternative was death.

It was Renia's mission, her responsibility, to witness and report. As she watched the ghetto burn, she snuck along the wall, trying to view the battle from as many points as possible. She did not let herself turn away.

She willed herself to view the battle for the promise it could deliver to the fighters in Będzin.

Others watched, too. Thousands of Poles and non-Jews stood on the sidelines, trying to make sense of what was happening. Renia returned to her hotel room, but she couldn't get the images she had seen out of her mind. All night, as she tried to sleep, Renia's bed shook from the bomb blasts.

Renia left for the train station in the early morning. She benefited from being underestimated and misjudged; she slipped out of Warsaw without anyone guessing what she was doing. To them, she was a simple Polish girl.

"Poles must be fighting alongside the Jews," she heard people on the train say. "There's simply no way that the Jews are capable of conducting such a heroic battle." Renia smiled to herself; that was a grand compliment to her people.

The train whizzed on, approaching the border. Renia was eager to share the news of the resistance and to inspire uprisings elsewhere. Next, Będzin!

FIFTEEN

Escape

May 1943

After the initial fighting, the Nazis changed their approach. Instead of armed combat, they decided to set the ghetto on fire.

It did not take long for the ghetto to burn. The Nazis destroyed one building at a time. After they set a building on fire, they chased any Jews who ran from their smoking hideouts and shot them; those who didn't run died in the blaze. Families and children frantically wandered through the crumbling streets, searching for shelter. The sky glowed with a terrifying red light. While this was going on, just outside the ghetto walls, some Poles enjoyed a spring day and visited a carousel with their children.

The Jewish Fighting Organization could no longer battle inside buildings or run across rooftops. The comrades had been ready to fight, but they had not imagined the possibility of intentionally being burned alive.

Zivia returned to the headquarters of the Jewish Fighting Organization, an enormous underground bunker. The central command lived there, along with a hundred and twenty fighters and other Jews who had been burned out of their shelters. The room had been built for several dozen people; it now housed more than three hundred. The air was stuffy. One comrade reported that it was impossible to light a candle because there was so little oxygen in the air.

During the day, the Jews remained still and quiet. At night, when the Nazis retired, the ghetto came alive. Zivia and the other comrades emerged from their shelters. Couriers made connections, fighters hunted for weapons and food.

Then, in the morning, the German soldiers returned.

Every night, the leadership of the Jewish Fighting Organization debated what to do. They could not remain in the burning ghetto. They sent messengers to hunt for hideouts outside the ghetto, but they had no success.

The leaders discussed their options. They had no outside help, few weapons, and the campaign was over. If they didn't make a move, they would starve to death waiting. Zivia suggested trying to escape through Warsaw's sewer system. Several fighters had already tried this, but they were either shot by the Nazis or they got lost underground. But Zivia knew they had no choice.

Zivia went with the first group on a sewage escape mission. First, the group had to sneak across the ghetto, wriggling on their bellies like snakes and later stepping over broken glass and charred corpses. Zivia led them to a guide who knew fourteen routes through the canals. The group left that night. Zivia stayed behind.

Each member jumped into the sewage water and began their escape. Two hours later, the guide returned and reported that the group made it out of the ghetto and climbed out of the manhole in the middle of the street. (Zivia didn't know it at the time, but they were discovered and attacked by the Germans. Hela, the courier, was the only survivor.)

The following night, Zivia returned to the headquarters to get the others to join the escape. When she reached the building, she saw the hidden entrances had been opened and no one was in sight. She later learned that the Germans fired poison gas into the bunker. The comrades held wet cloths over their mouths and noses, but it wasn't enough. Only a handful escaped from a hidden exit, and they were badly wounded.

Zivia's heart was shattered. *She should have been there.* But there was no time to mourn the dead. Zivia had to help those who were still alive. She had to figure out what to do next. Zivia set up a new headquarters. "Responsibility for others brings you back to your feet," Zivia later wrote, "despite everything." They arrived at the new bunker, carrying the wounded fighters.

Zivia sent another group off into the sewer canals. They soon returned to report that they'd met a Jewish fighter, Kazik, who had brought a Polish guide who could help them all get out. On May 9, a group of sixty fighters and civilians gathered with Zivia. Some comrades were badly injured and could not move; others could barely breathe from gas and smoke inhalation. She worried that there were more fighters in the ghetto, waiting for help. But the clock was ticking.

Zivia decided to save whoever she could.

She led the more able-bodied into the sewer. "It seemed as if you were leaping into the darkness of the depths, with the filthy water splashing and spraying about you," Zivia wrote. "You are overcome by a terrible feeling of nausea. Your legs are drenched with the foul-smelling cold slime of the sewer. But you keep on walking!"

In the sewers, Kazik and the guide took the lead, and Zivia followed in the rear. There were dozens of fighters, single file, dragging themselves through the sewage slime. The canals were dark and shallow; Zivia had to walk with her back stooped and her head bent. At some points, the foul water flowed neck-high and they had to hold their guns over their heads. Some parts were so narrow, it was hard for even one person to fit. The fighters were thirsty and hungry, and some carried their injured comrades.

Zivia remained overwhelmed by guilt and depression. She had to force herself to keep going. She kept thinking that she should have died with the others back at headquarters.

Miraculously, the entire group arrived before dawn at the sewer under Prosta Street in central Warsaw. It wasn't safe for them to exit. Kazik climbed out to find help. For an entire day, the group sat below the manhole, listening to the sounds of the street above—carriages, streetcars, and Polish children playing. In the middle of the afternoon, the manhole cover was opened and a note was thrown in. It said that the rescue would take place that night.

With that news, Zivia said, "Let's go back and bring the others!" She found two volunteers willing to bring the rest of the Jewish Fighting Organization to the canal entrance where they all waited.

At midnight, the manhole cover was raised, and soup and bread were lowered in. Still, they had to wait to get out because Kazik had not yet found a vehicle to transport them.

Early the following morning, the two fighters who had gone on the rescue mission returned, but they were alone. They reported that the Germans had sealed off all the canal openings and raised the water level through the entire sewage system, so they had to turn back.

At ten a.m., the manhole cover was raised and the Jews were told to hurry out. About forty people emerged from the sewer and climbed into a truck.

The truck driver was directed, at gunpoint, to listen to

instructions. Word came that there were Germans nearby. About twenty fighters had separated from the group and gone to a secondary location. Zivia wanted to wait for them; Kazik refused, saying it was too risky. He promised to send a truck later and ordered the driver to drive. Zivia was furious and threatened to shoot him. Ultimately, the truck left without the second group of fighters. For the rest of her life, Zivia was haunted by the knowledge that she hadn't waited for her comrades. (The second rescue attempt of the twenty remaining fighters failed. The Germans had found out about the morning's very public operation in the middle of the street and waited for the remaining fighters. Eventually the Jews climbed out, and were ambushed and killed.)

The truck ride out of Warsaw was difficult. Zivia lay on the cramped floor, silent, shocked, exhausted, filthy, and horrified about leaving people behind. The comrades stank. Their weapons were wet and useless. They had no idea where they were being taken.

After about an hour, they unloaded in a forest outside the city. They were met by other comrades, who were shocked that they were alive, and by their disheveled appearance.

Zivia drank hot milk and took in the greenery. For the first time in years, she began to weep. For too long she had been stoic and held her emotions inside; now, she let go.

The eighty surviving fighters gathered around a bonfire to regroup and to decide what to do next. There were Germans nearby, so they could not stay long. They made a register of all the weapons, money, and jewelry they had, and they built temporary shelters where they could pause, rest, and regroup. On that night, they felt as if they were the last Jews on earth.

SIXTEEN

Arms, Arms, Arms

May 1943

Back in Będzin, Frumka was relieved to hear Zivia was alive. But that joy turned to anguish when she learned that Hantze— her little sister—had been killed in the Warsaw ghetto. "I'm responsible," Frumka cried. "I'm the one who sent her to Warsaw."

The comrades had kept the news from her for as long as possible, but she needed to know the truth. She mourned and wailed, and eventually she accepted what she could not change. "But man is made of iron," Renia later wrote, "callous to suffering. Frumka returned to herself, even after this terrible blow."

Instead of weakness, Frumka vowed revenge. Frumka—and all the fighters in the Będzin group—dedicated themselves to fighting to the death. The six-week battle in Warsaw was the first urban uprising against the Nazis, of any underground anywhere. Fighters in every ghetto wanted to follow the example of the Warsaw Jewish fighters.

The underground's policy changed: all couriers had to travel in groups of two. Renia was paired with Ina Gelbart of The Young Guard. They both had papers allowing them to cross the border into the General Government.

In Warsaw they met their contact, Tarłów, a Jew with connections to forgers and weapons dealers. The revolvers and grenades that Renia would now smuggle came primarily from the Germans' weapons storehouses. Couriers got weapons from German army bases, weapons repair shops and factories, the black market, and the Polish resistance.

The girls found Tarłów without a problem, and he directed them to a cemetery. That's where they found what they wanted: guns, grenades, and explosives. Renia paid for the merchandise with money she pulled out of her shoe.

The Jewish resistance started in all the major ghettos with very few arms. In one ghetto, the underground had one rifle that had to be carried between units of fighters so each could train with a real weapon. In another, they shared one revolver and shot against a basement wall of mud so they could reuse the bullets. In Warsaw, the resistance had two pistols to start; in Kraków, the fighters first organized without a single gun.

The couriers went out to find and smuggle weapons and ammunition to the ghettos, often with little guidance, and always with tremendous risk. The courier girls' connections and expertise in hiding, bribing, and deflecting suspicion were critical. They didn't look the part of arms smugglers. One Freedom courier hid a revolver and two hand grenades inside a loaf of country bread in her suitcase. When a German policeman asked what she was carrying, she confessed that she had smuggled food. He didn't even open her bag. Instead, he told the train conductor to take care of her and make sure no one bothered her or her suitcase.

In another incident, Hela Schüpper went to Warsaw to buy guns. She dyed her hair bright blond and borrowed a stylish outfit from the mother of a non-Jewish friend. She looked like she was on her way to the theater. Instead, she approached a secret contact at the gate of a clinic. She was told he'd be reading a newspaper. Following instructions, she asked him for the time and to see his newspaper. He handed her the paper and walked away. Hela followed at a distance, getting on a different train car. They completed the deal, and she came away with five weapons, more than four pounds of explosives, and ammunition.

Courier Vladka Meed smuggled metal files into the Warsaw ghetto so Jews could cut through the window bars if they were trapped on a train to a death camp. Once, she had to repack three cartons of dynamite into smaller packages and pass them through the grate of a factory window in the subcellar of a building that bordered the ghetto. She bribed a non-Jewish guard to help her. When they finished, he was shaking and sweating and asked her what was in the packages. "Powdered paint," she said, careful to gather up some spilled dynamite from the floor.

Another courier smuggled grenades into the Warsaw ghetto in her underwear. When she had to take a crowded streetcar, a Pole offered her his seat. She was afraid to sit down because the bumpy ride could cause them all to explode. She chatted and flirted her way out of the situation, never giving a hint of her real fear, never sitting down.

After the Warsaw ghetto uprising, fighters needed weapons for defense and for future rebellions. Courier Leah Hammerstein worked as a kitchen helper in a hospital. One day when she passed a German soldier's empty room, she opened the closet and slipped his pistol under her dress. She walked to the bathroom and locked the door. She wrapped the gun in her underwear and pushed it out a window that opened onto the roof. Later, when she took out the trash, she went up to the roof, retrieved it, and threw it into the hospital garden. The gun was reported missing, and everyone searched the hospital, but she—a polite girl—wasn't a suspect. At the end of her shift, she picked the wrapped gun out of the weeds, put it in her purse, and went home.

* * *

After the meeting in the Warsaw cemetery, Renia and Ina returned to Będzin. They faced more surprise searches on this leg of their trip. Renia had guns strapped to her tiny body with fabric belts, and she carried a bag with a false bottom that concealed grenades and handmade explosive gasoline bombs. She tried to stay calm when the officer asked her what was in her bag; she admitted to having illegal potatoes. He took a few potatoes and let her go.

During the entire trip, Renia and Ina were prepared to do whatever was necessary for the mission. They had to be ready to jump from the train, stay calm during a search, and withstand torture. Some couriers carried cyanide powder sewn into the lining of their coat to kill themselves if they were caught.

Renia did not have cyanide, but she did have an iron will.

This was not quite the life she had imagined when she decided to become a stenographer.

SEVENTEEN

One Family

June 1943

At four a.m., Renia was awakened by the sound of gunshots in the distance. It should have been dark outside, but searchlights lit the streets and people ran outside, trying to find a way out. Police had surrounded the Będzin ghetto.

The Freedom leaders ordered most of the comrades to hide in the bunker. Nine fighters—those who had papers offering protection—were to remain in the house to reduce suspicion. If the Nazis found the building empty, they would search and find the group in hiding, and everyone would be killed.

Renia and the others who went into hiding crawled through the top of the stove and entered a prepared safe room. When they were all inside, one of the comrades who stayed behind secured the cover back on the stove.

An hour later, they heard the stomp of boots, voices cursing in German, closet doors opening, furniture tipping over. The Nazis were searching for them.

Renia and her comrades did not move. They barely breathed.

Finally, there was stillness. The Nazis were gone. But the comrades stayed silent for many more hours.

Nearly thirty people were stuffed inside the tiny bunker. The only fresh air flowed from a tiny crack in the wall. An unbearable heat set in. They waved their hands, trying to send air to each other, but it wasn't enough. One of the comrades collapsed. Fortunately, the group had stashed some water and smelling salts in the bunker, and they were able to revive her.

They waited more than seven hours. At last, someone came and lifted the stovetop. They were greeted by two comrades—the only two who survived—who told them that they had been driven to an empty lot and put into a long line. The Germans did not look at work certificates; they divided people into two groups: left and right, live and die. Those on one side were shipped to a death camp, the others were sent home. Some Jews tried to run, but they were shot in the back.

Renia and the others stepped outside. All around them, people were wailing. Everyone had someone—a mother or father, daughter or son, brother or sister, husband or wife—torn from them and taken. One of the comrades who disappeared that night was Hershel Springer, a beloved Freedom leader who was respected by the community.

They returned inside, unable to witness any more grief. Frumka pulled at her hair and banged her head in despair. "I am guilty!" she screamed. "Why did I tell them to stay in their rooms? I murdered them, I sent them to their deaths." Renia and the others tried to console her.

Renia headed toward the train station. The group to be deported stood in a line, guarded by armed soldiers. When the train arrived, the Nazis shoved people into overpacked cattle cars. There was not enough space, so the extra people were held in a large building that had once served as an orphanage and senior home. Renia watched as the wagons left for Auschwitz. The Jews being held would be sent out the following morning.

All aboard would be dead by the end of the day.

The Nazis needed several hundred more people to make up an even thousand. A few hours later, the Gestapo broke into a workshop and grabbed the remaining number. In two days, the Nazis took eight thousand people out of Będzin to be murdered, not counting those who were shot on the street or trying to run.

With Hershel gone, Frumka was no longer capable of running the kibbutz. She could not bear all the worry or plan for the future. She needed an opportunity to grieve. The comrades knew that it was only a matter of time until they'd all be killed.

They considered leaving the ghetto and dividing into groups.

Several days later—just when they needed a miracle—Renia received a note. It was in Hershel's handwriting. Could it be real?

Renia and two other comrades followed an escort to a hidden storage room in a factory, where they saw Hershel. He had been badly beaten and his feet were wounded. He hugged Renia like a father and told them about his escape. "They shoved us into the train car . . . I looked for a way to escape," Hershel told Renia. He had a pocket knife and a chisel with him, which he used to pry open a window. When he was about to jump out of the train, the other Jews held his arms and legs, screaming, "What are you doing? . . . Because of you they'll kill us like cattle."

He waited and when the group was distracted, he climbed up and jumped. Others jumped behind him. "I preferred to die this way than to end my life in Auschwitz," he said. Hershel heard gunshots from the Germans who were guarding the road. He hid in a pit, and the train moved on. A Polish woman working in the field spotted him and pulled him away from the tracks.

His feet were hurt, and he couldn't walk. The woman told him that Auschwitz was nearby, and he was smart to jump. She brought him food and bandaged his foot. She warned him that the people in the village would hand him over to the Germans, so she told him which way to go. That night, he began crawling in the direction she suggested. He ate carrots and beets from the fields he passed. "After a week of crawling," Hershel said, "I arrived here."

Renia brought Hershel back to the kibbutz. Frumka and the others were overjoyed to see him. It was as if he had returned from the dead. At least for the moment, they felt things might turn out okay.

Of course, their joy was temporary. The comrades learned that the police had become suspicious of their kibbutz's activities. The Freedom comrades divided into three ten-member units and moved to different parts of the ghetto. Despite the separate living spaces, they kept their connection strong. "We are all one family" was the motto that guided them, always.

EIGHTEEN

Freedom in the Forests

June 1943

In late spring 1943, blond-haired, blue-eyed Freedom member Marek Folman arrived in Będzin. Renia listened to his stories of serving with a partisans unit, an armed group formed to fight against the occupying German army. Based in the forest, he had helped attack German barracks, plant mines under military trains, and burn government buildings.

Marek had come to Będzin to encourage Jewish fighters to join a local partisan unit. He said he knew a Polish officer, Socha, who would help them make the necessary connections.

The entire kibbutz was excited. Initially, they had wanted

to fight as Jews in the ghetto, but they knew their options were limited. Joining the forest partisans offered a way to act.

They didn't trust Socha at first. Two comrades went to his apartment to learn more. He appeared to be from a typical Polish working-class family: the modest home was filled with babies crying for food and being tended to by a peasant wife. After meeting his family, they agreed to go with him.

The Jewish Fighting Organization sent several men from each of their movements. The plan was that they would escape from the ghetto, remove their Jewish stars, meet Socha at an agreed-upon spot, then follow him into the forest. They promised to write home when they arrived.

A few weeks later, the comrades heard that Socha had returned to town. Marek went to his apartment, where he was told that the comrades had arrived safely and had gone out to fight the same day. They had simply forgotten to write.

Pleased with the news of success, a second group followed. Renia begged to join the group, but she was needed as a courier. The fighters going to the forest had taken almost all the weapons with them, so Renia still had work to do. She was privately disappointed, but of course abided by orders, wanting to contribute to the resistance however best she could.

A few days after the second group left Będzin to go to the forest, one of the comrades returned. He was weak and barely able to walk. He told Renia and the others that Socha had led them for six hours, then he urged them to rest and eat because they were no longer in danger of being caught by the Germans. He gave them water and said he was going to check on their location.

A moment later, they were surrounded by German soldiers on horseback. The Germans shot at the fighters. "I'd been sitting under a bush, so I fell but wasn't injured," the comrade said. "I managed to stay alive. But the Nazis killed everyone else." They then robbed the corpses of whatever they had in their pockets. "One German lifted my leg, satisfied I'd been murdered," he said. "After they left, I crawled out of my spot and ran."

They had trusted Socha, but he had been working for the Nazis. Twenty-five comrades were dead. There were barely enough people left to fight.

Marek was insane with remorse. He wanted to die. He slipped out of the ghetto alone, and no one ever saw him again.

While the fighters in Będzin had been betrayed, there were other Jews who were able to join the forest partisans, although it wasn't easy. A number of groups fought from the woods, and though each had its own philosophy, they all rarely accepted Jews. Some partisans were antisemitic; others didn't think Jews were good soldiers. Most Jews joining the fight had no weapons or military training, and they were in physical and mental distress. They were considered a burden. Women weren't considered fighters; they were thought to be useful only for cooking, cleaning, and nursing.

Still, about thirty thousand Jews did enroll in forest partisan units, often hiding their identity, or having to prove themselves by working twice as hard. Of these, about three thousand were women.

Life in the forest was especially difficult for Jewish women. Some Polish groups suspected Jewish women of being Nazi spies. Many women had to become romantically involved with men they didn't care for because they were dependent on them for survival. For the most part, Jewish women were forced to cook, wash, and make leather boots for the male fighters who carried the guns. In unit headquarters, women were clerks, stenographers, and translators, and a handful were doctors and nurses.

A few exceptional women were chosen to be intelligence agents, lookouts, weapon transporters, and saboteurs. One such woman was Faye Schulman, a photographer from the eastern border town Lenin. She had been spared from a mass shooting because of her artistic skill. Eventually, Faye fled to the woods and convinced a Soviet partisan unit to let her join. She was ordered to become a nurse, even though she knew nothing about medicine. She was trained by a veterinarian and performed open-air surgeries on an operating table made of branches. She was a fighter who went out on missions. Her gun was her pillow. She was nineteen.

* * *

Many Jews serving with partisan units kept their religion a secret. Unless that is, they joined a resistance unit made up entirely of Jews. These unique detachments were usually established by Jewish leaders in the dense forests in the eastern part of Poland. They were primarily family camps that sheltered Jewish refugees and also committed acts of sabotage.

One of them was called "The Avengers" and comprised youth from Vilna, including Young Guard comrades Ruzka Korczak and Vitka Kempner.

After her town was overrun by Nazis back in 1939, Ruzka had traveled three hundred miles to Vilna, where she moved into a poorhouse that housed a thousand teenagers. She was a good listener and problem solver, and she quickly became a youth leader.

One morning, as tiny Ruzka was reading a thick book, she was approached by a bouncy girl who spoke perfect Polish. "Why such a serious book?" the girl asked.

"The world is a serious place," Ruzka said. And Ruzka was a serious girl. She was a shy outsider who loved to read; she spent her free time in the library.

"I think the world is not so serious," the other girl, Vitka, said. She then explained that even if it is, "all the more reason not to read a serious book."

Vitka was a free spirit who had fled her small town by climbing out the bathroom window of the synagogue where the Nazis had locked all the Jews. A top student at Jewish school, Vitka considered herself a Polish patriot.

Ruzka and Vitka became best friends. Ruzka was serious; Vitka was carefree. One day they noticed a young man watching the comrades in the poorhouse. Vitka approached him and introduced herself to Abba Kovner, an attractive leader of The Young Guard. The three became close and later lived together in the ghetto. They helped initiate the Vilna underground, called the United Partisan Organization; they helped gather weapons and plan a revolt.

Abba sent Vitka on a mission to blow up a German train carrying soldiers and supplies. For two weeks Vitka left the ghetto in the evenings, hunting for the best location for a bomb. She studied the tracks, taking note of all the details since the act would have to be carried out in the dark of night.

More than once Vitka was stopped by Germans policing the tracks. "I'm just looking for my way home," Vitka said. "I had no idea it was forbidden to walk here." Each time, they let her go.

Once, forced to change her route, Vitka stumbled into a German shooting range. She was nearly gunned down. She pretended to be lost and approached a Nazi in tears. The soldier tried to help and ordered two others to walk her out. She later claimed that whenever she was in danger, she felt an "icy calm" and was able assess the situation and get out safely.

Finally, on a warm July night, Vitka slipped out of the ghetto with two boys and a girl. Under their jackets they carried pistols, grenades, a pipe bomb, and a detonator. Vitka led the group to the perfect spot that she'd identified. They secured the bomb to the tracks, then hid in the woods. They set off the bomb, and the train derailed!

The Germans immediately began to fire. They hit the girl who had come with Vitka, who buried her in the forest, then ran back to the ghetto before dawn. Though blowing up trains would become a common goal for the Polish resistance, Vitka's was the first such act of sabotage in Occupied Europe.

A few days later an underground newspaper reported that Polish fighters blew up a train and killed more than two hundred German soldiers. In response, the Germans killed sixty peasants in the nearest town as punishment. "This is not something I felt guilty about," Vitka later said. "I knew that it was not me killing these people—it was the Germans."

The Jews in the Vilna ghetto did not support a grand ghetto battle, and after a small confrontation, instead of fighting, Vitka helped two hundred comrades escape to the forest to fight. Abba became the commander of a Jewish brigade, split into four divisions. He was the leader of the Avenger unit. Vitka commanded her own scouting troupe. Ruzka became the patrol unit commander.

Ruzka was selected to go on the initial sabotage operation, along with four men. They were to hike forty miles and blow up a munitions train. They set out in the early evening in the freezing cold, each one carrying a gun and two grenades. Ruzka insisted on taking her turn carrying the mine, which weighed more than fifty pounds. When they were crossing over a river, the group had to inch along a log. Ruzka fell in. She caught the log and hauled herself up, even though her legs were numb and heavy. The commander told her to go back to camp so she wouldn't freeze to death.

"You will have to put a bullet in my head to keep me from this mission," she said. Instead of turning back, the group broke into a peasant's home and stole dry clothes for Ruzka. The men's clothes were too big, so she had to cuff the sleeves and pants and stuff the boots with extra socks. They successfully completed their mission, and a storehouse of German weapons was destroyed.

A group of Soviet partisans wanted to target a German city. They had weapons, but they needed information. They approached Abba Kovner and asked "to borrow a few Jewish girls." Instead, Abba suggested that it should be a Jewish mission, and the Russians should give them the weapons.

Two men and two women left the Jewish camp dressed as peasants. One of the women—Vitka—carried an old suitcase containing magnetic mines and time bombs that could stick to any metal surface. The group headed into the hills around Vilna, and paused at the fur factory in a forced labor camp. Vitka spoke to Sonia Madejsker, a Jewish communist who lived in the camp and was their last link to the underground in Vilna. Sonia said that the factory was soon going to be shut down, and the Jews would be sent to their execution. The workers wanted to flee with Vitka to the forest, where they might have a chance at survival.

The Soviet commander was upset by the number of Jews living in their camps as refugees, who all needed food and clothes. So Vitka said she was there as a soldier, not a humanitarian. Sonia explained that if Vitka didn't take the people, they would die.

First, Vitka had to carry out her mission. She decided that the men would blow up the waterworks (the city's sewers and taps), while the women took out the electrical transformers (the city's lighting system). At dusk, both groups set off for their targets. The men planted a bomb in a manhole. The women made it to the transformers, but the mines, which were covered in paint, would not stick. Vitka furiously scratched away the paint until her fingers bled. The timers were set for four hours.

They regrouped at the labor camp. The men were tired and wanted to rest that night in the factory. Vitka insisted that after the bombs went off, security would be tightened and it would be dangerous to travel. Vitka knew they were running out of time. She told Sonia to bring her all the people who were ready to leave; she was taking them to the forest immediately. The boys stayed.

Within an hour, Vitka was leading a group of sixty Jews down dark roads, out of the city. They heard the bombs explode and saw the city go black.

The next day, the men who stayed behind were caught.

* * *

Ruzka, Vitka, and the Jewish resistance fighters continued their work through the difficult winter. They blew up vehicles and bridges, and invented bombs that were safer to use. Partisans used their bare hands to rip down telephone poles, telegraph wires, and train tracks.

One April morning, Vitka left for a mission in Vilna. She carried a list of medicines and a plea for the Communist rebels of the city to revolt. While she was walking, an elderly peasant asked if she could join her for the journey. As they crossed a bridge, the old woman whispered to the soldiers standing guard that Vitka was a Jew, no doubt hoping to earn a reward for her capture.

The guards looked at Vitka's ID papers. "They're false."

Vitka ripped the plea for the rebels to shreds and threw them in the air, but the peasant woman grabbed the pieces and handed them to the soldiers. They took Vitka to the Gestapo.

Vitka quickly assessed the situation and changed her approach. "You're right," she said. "I am a Jew and a Partisan. That is why you should let me go." She explained that the Nazis were losing, and whoever killed her would themselves soon be killed. She also explained that many police officers were cooperative with the resistance. It worked: one of the policemen took her aside, shoved her fake ID back into her hand, and told her he hoped to meet her commander. He instructed her never to cross that bridge again.

When she came back to camp, Vitka said that that had been her last mission. "It is a miracle that I made it back," she said. "How often can a person depend on miracles?"

NINETEEN

After the Ghettos

July 1943

In the summer of 1943, Renia knew the end of the Będzin ghetto was coming. For the most part, the youth of the resistance movement no longer dreamed of a grand battle. Too many fighters and friends had already died. Some held on, still insisting on a revolt, but most simply wanted to flee and survive.

Frumka and Hershel decided to send the orphans out first. The children with lighter hair and eyes were prepared to go to German farms. Renia and her comrades altered documents for them, covering up old data with false information and fingerprints. When they were ready, the children were snuck out of the ghetto and taken to the town council of a rural village, where they told officials that they had no parents and wanted to work. Many farmers welcomed the cheap labor. Placements were found for eight children.

The children who looked the most Jewish remained in the ghetto.

Zivia wrote to the Będzin group from her hiding spot in Warsaw. She urged them to give up their dreams of rebellion. After the Warsaw ghetto uprising, she no longer promoted fighting; she decided the death toll wasn't worth it. Instead, Zivia said, if they wanted to stay alive, they should come to Warsaw. She said that people who didn't look Jewish could probably get by with false papers. Those who looked Jewish could hide and try to wait out the rest of the war.

The courier girls helped Jews relocate from ghettos and camps. They supplied them with false papers and found them apartments and hiding places inside homes, barns, and factories. They often paid the room and board to the Poles who hid them.

In Warsaw, the couriers occasionally visited those they were helping, bringing them news and moral support. They dealt with blackmailers who threatened to turn in hidden Jews unless they were paid off, and as a result couriers often had to move Jews from one covert location to another. They did this while keeping up their own disguised lives as well.

Courier Vladka Meed snuck children out of the ghetto

before it was demolished. They were a priority: the Nazis killed children because they represented the Jewish future. It was difficult work. The children had to take on new names and identities. They had to speak proper Polish, not ask questions, and keep quiet about their former life in the ghetto. And they had to be able to leave their families.

Vladka became a courier for a rescue organization that helped twelve thousand Jews in the Warsaw area. An estimated twenty thousand to thirty thousand Jews remained in hiding in the city. Vladka's work spread by word of mouth. To receive aid, Jews had to submit a written application detailing their position and their "budgets." Most applicants were the sole survivors of their families, having run from camps or jumped off trains. The types of requests varied: an oral surgeon requested dental instruments so he could work, another man asked for money to support his orphaned niece and nephew, a young newspaper delivery boy asked for a heavy coat so he could work in the winter months. The courier girls often delivered monthly funds, visited the children, and made new arrangements when plans backfired, as they often did.

Over time, hiding places had to become more creative. In one apartment, a wall was built next to a toilet to create a secret space. In another home, a Jew was hidden inside a hollow tiled stove. Thirty Jews lived in a suburban hideout under a garden. Some Jews secured larger spaces, but they were not free of the anxiety and depression caused by being confined.

Vladka maintained connections with Hungarian smugglers, with Polish resistance fighters, and with Jews outside Warsaw. On one mission, she tried to help a group of Jewish fighters who were hiding with peasants in the countryside. On the train she pretended to be a Polish smuggler. She later found the comrades she was looking for and brought them cash, clothes, and medication on a regular basis. Once, funds were delayed and she arrived later than expected, only to find that the hidden Jews had been evicted. Some had been killed, but others had joined Polish partisan units or hid in the forests.

While doing this work, the couriers had to maintain the fiction of their own identities. All they could hope to do was stay one step ahead of the informants and blackmailers. In Warsaw, Vladka moved around often. At one point she rented a small apartment that had been handed to her from another Jewish courier. She immediately created places for hiding materials, like a valise with a double bottom and a ladle with a hollow handle. The neighbors found out that the former tenant was Jewish and began to suspect Vladka. She worried that if she left, it would increase their suspicion and undermine the false Christian identity she had spent so long creating. She stayed and arranged for a Polish friend to visit and pretend to be her mother. She also invited her neighbors over for tea to prove she had nothing to hide. Some Jews mailed themselves letters from nearby towns to make it seem that they had Polish friends and family.

Like Vladka, roughly thirty thousand Jews survived by

"passing" as non-Jews. Most of them were young, single, middle- and upper-middle-class women with fake identifications and Polish-looking complexions. Sometimes parents urged their children to flee and "live for their family." These women were actors: they often felt they could play the role because they had previously been mistaken as non-Jews. Those who maintained a Jewish social circle tended to fare better psychologically because they had time to rest from the constant performance. They had friends who knew their true identity.

Zivia looked too Jewish to go out on the street. When she was in hiding, she had a lot of time on her hands. For many, it was difficult to be locked away with people who weren't necessarily friends. Every knock on the door caused those in hiding to run for cover. Zivia spent her time writing letters. She pleaded with the Będzin group to flee instead of fight—the loss of life was too much to bear.

Zivia began to work for a relief organization like Vlad-ka's, where she organized the distribution of money and fake documents. Once again, she dispatched "Zivia's girls" on around-the-clock missions to connect, inform, and protect Jews. She also sent out courier girls to look for fighters who were in trouble, and once in a while, to locate other couriers who'd mysteriously gone missing.

TWENTY

Missed Connection

July 1943

When the Będzin Jewish Fighting Organization received Zivia's letters, they organized an escape. People who could pass as non-Jewish would travel to Warsaw by train. Those who couldn't pass would be smuggled to Warsaw on a bus. To achieve their goal, they needed forged documents for the travelers. They had some of the documents, but two couriers—Renia and Ina—were to collect the rest.

Ina and Renia divided the money, photographs, and list of addresses for the counterfeiter. Ina left for Warsaw one night, and Renia the following morning. Renia also escorted twenty-two-year-old Rivka Moscovitch, a Freedom fighter who had become sick. She had badly wanted to stay and fight, but the group knew she would do better recovering in Warsaw and then helping to find hiding places for other Jews.

Before leaving, Renia and Ina had agreed on a time and place to meet in the city. Renia and Rivka pretended to be two Polish girls taking a trip to the big city. Forcing smiles, they made it through the difficult checkpoints without raising suspicion, even though Rivka was sick.

They arrived in Warsaw, exhausted. When they went to meet Ina, she was not there. How long could they wait? It looked suspicious. Had Ina been arrested on the way?

Renia had no other addresses. She only had enough money for one more day. She had to take Rivka somewhere, so they went to the inn where Renia had planned to stay. She left her traveling companion to rest and went out to figure out what to do. She went to see the sister of an acquaintance from Będzin and asked if she knew the address of a former youth group friend. In a stroke of good fortune, the woman was able to give Renia the address of his mother.

She returned to the meeting place, but still no Ina.

The next morning, Renia took Rivka to see the mother of her old Freedom comrade. The entire family had supported the Jewish Fighting Organization, but the comrade's mother explained that she could not keep Rivka in her home because Nazis knocked on her door every day. Instead, Rivka was taken to the home of a sympathetic Polish neighbor.

The comrade's mother helped Renia connect with Antek, Zivia's boyfriend. Renia wore a dress, new shoes, and a red flower in her braided hair, the sign for him to recognize her. Renia went to the designated spot and saw a man with a folded newspaper under his arm, his sign. He was tall and blond, dressed in a green outfit.

She walked by, making sure to slow down and show her flower.

He didn't move.

She turned and walked past him again.

Still nothing.

Was it the wrong man? Did he know they were being watched?

Her gut told her to take a chance. "Hello," Renia offered in Polish. "Are you Antek?"

"Are you Wanda?" he asked, referring to her fake name.

"Yes."

Neither had thought the other could possibly have been Jewish.

As they spoke, she could hear it in his Polish accent: he sounded like a Jew from Vilna.

The man said he had no news about what had happened to Ina, but he hoped she was just delayed. He promised to arrange for the false documentation as quickly as possible, but it would take some time.

Rivka was moved to a safe house.

Renia waited in Warsaw for several days. She knew the final deportation from Będzin was going to happen imminently. The clock was ticking, so she took what she could get and decided to return. She traveled home with twenty-two false visas taped to her body and sewn into her skirt.

On the train, Renia tried to look casual, as if she wasn't carrying illegal material. She smiled and remained calm, even though she wondered what had happened to Ina.

Only later did she learn that Ina had been caught by a female Nazi guard at a checkpoint near the border. The Gestapo decided to drive her to Auschwitz, but Ina jumped out of the car and ran. She made her way to a friend in a local ghetto. The Nazis put a high price on her head: either Ina would be surrendered or twenty Jews would be killed. The Jewish police found her and handed her over. She died before she reached Auschwitz.

TWENTY-ONE

Nothing Left to Lose

August 1943

On August 1, 1943, Renia arrived in Będzin, dirty, broken, and exhausted. When she stepped off the train, she entered a scene of absolute chaos. Nazis were chasing the passengers away from the station. In the distance—in the direction of the ghetto—Renia heard screams and turmoil.

"What's happening?" Renia asked the Poles who were gathered nearby.

"They've been taking Jews out of the city since Friday," they said. "One group after another."

It was Monday, the fourth day. And it was not the end.

"Will they expel all the Jews?" Renia asked. She tried to sound unconcerned, pretending not to care, as if the people she loved were not all trapped inside. This was the moment she had dreaded for months. She had no idea if she would see her sister or her friends again.

The ghetto was surrounded by Nazis and police. There was no way to enter. Renia watched and listened, trying to piece together what was happening. Inside the ghetto, Germans were exposing bunkers and murdering people on the spot. Other Jews were being pushed into cattle cars and taken to death camps. Outside the ghetto, Germans hunted on the streets like wild dogs, checking documents, looking for more victims.

Renia recognized some friends in a group of people being held at gunpoint near the station. She didn't see her sister. She was watching those she cared for being driven to their death. Was she the only surviving Freedom courier?

At that point, Renia's life seemed pointless. "In my heart I thought: My life has lost all meaning. Why live, now that they have taken everything from me—my family, my relatives, and now my beloved friends?" She thought about killing herself. "An inner demon told me to put an end to my own life," Renia recalled. "And then I felt shame for this weakness. No! I will not ease the Germans' work with my own hands!"

Instead, she turned her thoughts to survival and revenge.

Renia began to walk. She had no home, no direction. She decided to go back to Warsaw, but the next train didn't leave until five a.m. the next day.

* * *

Renia walked all day. She had eaten nothing for as long as she could remember. She tried to think of someone—anyone—who might be willing to help her. Suddenly, she remembered a dentist, Dr. Weiss, who lived about four miles west of Będzin.

After jumping on and off trains and tramways to avoid document checks, she arrived in the town. Again she found the Jewish ghetto surrounded by Nazis. The expulsion was happening here, too.

Renia made her way to the dentist's home and knocked on the door. Dr. Weiss, a Russian woman, opened the door and stared at Renia in shock. "How did you get here?"

She offered Renia a chair, afraid she would collapse. Then she went to the kitchen to make tea.

Renia wanted to tell Dr. Weiss everything, but she couldn't speak. Instead, she began to cry in wild, convulsive sobs.

Dr. Weiss patted her head. "Don't cry," she said. "You have always been brave. I hold you up as a hero. Your courage is an example for me. You must be strong, my child. Maybe some of your people are still alive."

Renia felt she had reached her limit. "My heart wanted to die," she later wrote. Renia calmed down. She needed to rest and regroup to stay alive.

Dr. Weiss gave her some tea. "I would love for you to spend the night in my home," Dr. Weiss said. "But the Germans often break into houses out of nowhere, searching for hidden Jews. If they're in the area, they'll surely come here. I'm Russian. They

145

already suspect me of maintaining connections with Jews."

Renia could barely believe what she was hearing.

"Forgive me," Dr. Weiss said, "but I cannot risk my life."

Renia was lost. Where could she spend the night? She knew no one else in town.

Dr. Weiss gave her some food for the road. She blessed her, tears in her eyes, and said again, "I'm so sorry."

Alone, Renia left the city and walked toward the forest to find shelter for the night. At some point in the night, a man appeared out of nowhere and approached her. He was drunk and sat down near her. She moved away, and he moved closer. Sexual violence against women was common during the Holocaust, and Renia had no one to protect or defend her.

The man yelled at her. Despite her exhaustion, Renia jumped up and ran as fast as she could.

The man ran after her.

She ran until she reached a farmhouse. She found an open door, slipped inside the building, and crouched under the stairwell.

In the morning, Renia, tortured and weary, went to the train station and left for Warsaw.

PART THREE

"No Border Will Stand in Their Way"

"They are ready for anything and no border will stand in their way."

—Chaika Grossman,
on the movement's women, *Women in the Ghettos*

TWENTY-TWO

The Bunker and Beyond

August 1943

Once she reached Warsaw, Renia was distraught. She thought she might lose her mind waiting for news from Będzin. What happened to her friends, her loves, her sister? She needed to know where things stood so she could plan her next steps.

It took three weeks, but at last a postcard arrived from seventeen-year-old comrade Ilza Hansdorf. "Come to Będzin immediately," the postcard said. "I'll explain everything once you get here."

Within hours, Renia was packing for her trip. The underground provided her with a false travel permit, as well as two extra ones in case anyone else was still alive in Będzin. Renia was also given money for food, shelter, and the unexpected.

Renia went to the address listed on the postcard. It was the home of Mrs. Novak, the wife of a Polish mechanic who had helped at the kibbutz's laundry. He had assisted the Freedom comrades throughout the war.

When the door opened she saw two people—Meir and Nacha Schulman—who were not members of the movement but had been friends. Meir knew a lot about technology and had helped Freedom build their bunkers and install secret radios. He cleaned and repaired their broken weapons and attempted to produce counterfeit money.

Renia was pleased to know the Schulmans had survived, and she hoped they could answer her questions: Where is everyone? What happened to the fighters? How is my sister Sarah?

Eventually, Renia learned several versions of what had happened to the youth movement fighters left behind. One of the most complete was the story told by Chajka, the serious young woman who was one of the last fighters left standing in Będzin.

According to Chajka, the Nazis entered the ghetto at three o'clock on a Sunday morning. The comrades were awakened, caught completely unprepared. They had a few guns, but most of their weapons had been left at a different location. They were almost empty-handed.

They went downstairs and snatched two loaves of bread and

a pot of water, and then about twenty comrades entered their bunker through the oven door.

The shelter was small and unfinished. The only fresh air came from a small hole in the appliance.

The Nazis searched for them. From inside the bunker, the comrades heard the Germans trying to tear apart the floor above them, and even trying to open the oven. It was only a matter of time until they would be captured.

They had no ability to communicate with the other Jewish Fighting Organization hideouts. They feared they were the last Jews. Despite the risk, their leader Zvi Brandes decided to slip out and check on the Freedom kibbutz. The group felt relief when he returned, but they soon ran out of water. Zvi and another comrade left again, this time to collect supplies.

People were growing weaker and weaker. The next day, when Zvi slipped out to help his thirsty comrades, the tap was dry. The Nazis had cut the water supply.

Zvi decided they needed to move to the Freedom kibbutz bunker. Some of the comrades, including Chajka, left in the first wave. On the way, rockets fell on the entire street. She managed to crawl to a nearby building and eventually made it to the Freedom kibbutz. There were twenty or more people there.

The new hiding place—where Meir and Nacha Schulman and Renia's sister Sarah had also found refuge—was worse than the one Chajka had left. They had only two guns. The air was stuffy; everyone was hot and sweaty.

Chajka couldn't stand staying in the bunker. *I want to breathe my last on the surface, look up at the sky once more, and swallow my fill of water and air*, she thought. At night the leaders opened the hatch, and Chajka left with several other comrades.

They heard shots and had to retreat. She saw searchlights and observation posts. She didn't see a way out. The Nazis were launching a full-fledged war against thirsty, unarmed Jews in bunkers. It was impossible.

They decided that they were going to die waiting, so they should try to get out. They planned to have several people try to escape each day, but no one wanted to; no one wanted to leave the group.

One comrade went to gather information. Hours later, he returned, reporting that a few Jews remained and were working in a liquidation camp that had been set up to clear the ghetto of Jewish possessions.

Suddenly, they heard shouting in German. The hatch opened.

They'd been discovered.

The Nazis ordered them to come out. Then, one of them found the fighters' gun. This was the end. A moment later one of the comrades came down and said, "They've arranged everyone on the ground and [they] threaten to execute everybody unless you come out."

Silence.

"I'll be the sacrifice," said Zvi. "I'll go."

Chajka climbed out next. Meir and Nacha remained inside.

"Is there anybody else in there?" a Nazi asked.

They sent Hershel to check. "Nobody's there." He would not give away Meir and Nacha.

The Germans ordered them all to stand and march. One of the comrades was crying and pleading.

"You idiot, calm down," Chajka said. "Have some dignity."

Later, Renia also heard the story of what happened at a different bunker known as "the fighters' bunker." Frumka and six other Freedom comrades were staying in this well-camouflaged cellar, which was finely constructed, with an entrance concealed in the wall. It was equipped with electricity, water, and heat.

The fighters could hear German voices coming from above them. One of the comrades snapped and called out: "Let's retaliate before we fall!" He cocked his gun and fired through a small crack. Two Germans fell to the ground.

Of course, the shots drew attention. Germans rushed to the house, without getting too close. They carried away the two Nazi corpses, shocked to find Jews who still wanted to fight.

Frumka held her weapon. "Practice caution," she said. "But kill a few and die an honorable death." The comrades cocked their guns and fired.

Dozens of Nazis ambushed the house with grenades and

smoke bombs. Inside the bunker, the haze from the bombs and the burning house above them made their eyes sting. They began to suffocate. The Germans used a special pump to fill the bunker with water and drown them all.

When Frumka's body was found, she was still clutching a revolver.

When the smoke cleared, the ghetto was deserted. The deportation had been going on for a week. Some Jews had tried to escape. A few had been sent to work camps; a small number were kept to clear the ghetto apartments. Those waiting to be deported were held in a building. Chajka and the resistance group were forced to sit on the ground outside without moving.

Jews tried to bribe Germans to get work placements, but they had nothing left to bribe them with.

The Nazis called Chajka and another comrade. She expected to be executed. "Farewell," she said, strutting boldly, head up.

The Nazis took her to a former militia building and told her to wait outside while the other comrade went in.

"What are you doing here?" asked a clerk who was walking past.

"Nothing really," Chajka said. "They want to execute me."

"How come? What for?"

"They found something in our bunker."

The man was carrying a tray of apples. Chajka casually took one and bit into it. The man looked at her as if she were out of her mind. When she was called into the building, she threw the apple core down and rehearsed the line she planned to say in her final moment: "Murderers, your day of reckoning will come. Our blood will be avenged. Your end is already near."

As Chajka walked toward what she assumed would be her execution site, she thought about screaming, but no one would hear her. She remained calm and silent.

She saw her comrade in the corner. She had been beaten, but she was alive.

The Nazis began to beat Chajka. "Say whose gun this is, and we'll leave you alone," they shouted.

"I don't know," Chajka answered. "I'm innocent. Mama, Mama."

Finally, he stopped and moved back to the other comrade. When they tired of beating her, they returned to Chajka.

She overheard the word "Auschwitz." Then she and the other comrade were dragged back to the group. She was bruised and in pain and she curled up on the ground.

Without warning, Zvi sprang to his feet and ran.

The soldiers began shooting and running after him.

Then they returned. "Already done!" one of them said. "I got him!"

In the dark, Chajka promised herself that she would never go to Auschwitz. She would run, jump, or shoot herself first.

In the morning, the comrades were again denied food and water. At last a German guard took pity on them and ordered them to get up. He gave them a little something to eat and drink.

Nazis came over and took four men. Were they going to be executed?

They came back carrying Zvi's body.

Chajka's heart broke inside her, but she said nothing.

Ten times a day, they thought the Germans were coming to kill them. "[The] waiting was worse than death," Chajka wrote. In the evening, an order came. Tomorrow she was to be sent to Auschwitz.

The next morning, Jews grabbed their towels and washed their faces, as if this were a normal day. Chajka wanted them to revolt, to run, to fight.

Just before they were to leave, a flurry of people came through the area. Chajka knew this was it. After a moment's hesitation, she walked over to the kitchen of the liquidation camp, away from the group going to the death camp. A soldier stood in front of the door. She did not know why, but he let her in.

Several other comrades, including Renia's sister Sarah, joined Chajka in the kitchen.

Chajka expected to be sent back to the Auschwitz group because of her face. Instead, the commander looked at Chajka for a long time, then shook his head. "New faces," he said. "But [okay], they should stay."

At ten a.m., the transports left for Auschwitz. This time, Chajka had been spared.

*   *   *

When Renia returned to Będzin, Chajka was alive and working in the camp kitchen, preparing food for the people who
were liquidating the Jewish apartments. She was the last surviving leader of The Young Guard and the Będzin resistance.
The other Jews wanted Chajka to run away because they were
afraid they'd all be killed if the Gestapo remembered who she
was. Whenever the Nazi who had beat her entered the quarters,
Chajka hid under the bathtub.

Chajka also worked at the building where the murdered
Jews' possessions were collected. The objects were curated like a
gallery. There were barracks for pots, glassware, silk, silverware,
and other valuables. German women wearing stolen Jewish
suits, furs, and jewelry came to the camp to select objects for
their families. Chajka was sickened by this.

In time, the soldiers who had been stationed in Będzin were
ordered to the front. When the new German soldiers arrived,
Chajka befriended them. They didn't believe the stories of mass
murder. She began the mission she was given by The Young
Guard to spread the word; in this case, she enlightened the Germans and told them exactly what they were doing.

TWENTY-THREE

The Gestapo Net

August 1943

When Renia learned that some of her comrades—including her sister Sarah—were at the liquidation camp, she was desperate to figure out a way to free them. Each day more Jews were deported to death, so she had to act as soon as possible.

After asking everyone she knew, she learned she might get help from Bolk Kojak, a member of The Zionist Youth, a less political youth group that focused on Jewish rescue. Bolk had been friends with several Freedom members, and he knew a few of the camp guards.

Renia and her friend Ilza spent two days waiting to meet

him. When they finally met, they walked together down the street, then sat together on a bench. "Please help me," Renia begged. They kept their voices low because there were two older Polish women sitting nearby.

"My priority is to rescue members of The Zionist Youth," he said.

Renia did not let up. She pleaded for help—and she offered him several thousand German marks if he saved even one of her comrades.

"Meet me again, the day after tomorrow," he said. "Six a.m."

They parted: Bolk going one way, Renia and Ilza another. The women hurried to catch a tram to a nearby town, where they were going to spend the night. Suddenly, the two women who'd been sitting near them on the bench appeared. "You're Jewish, aren't you?" one woman accused.

They were followed by a group of children yelling, "Jews, Jews!"

Ilza wanted to run, but Renia didn't want to raise suspicion. They walked to an empty building, but they were now being followed by a crowd of people. "You're disguised as Poles," one of the older women yelled. "You met with a Jewish man."

A mob gathered around them. "We should kill you Hebrews, all of you," someone yelled. "If Hitler doesn't get the job done, we will," said another.

Without thinking, Renia lifted her arm and slapped the old woman across the face again and again. "If I'm actually a Jew,"

Renia said between whacks, "you should know what a Jew is capable of. Call me a Jew again," she threatened, "and you'll get more of the same."

Two undercover Gestapo agents arrived at the scene. "What's going on?" they asked.

Renia told them the story in Polish, and a boy from the street translated. "The woman is not in her right mind if she suspects that I am a Jew," Renia said, calm, then whipped out their fingerprinted papers. "Check our documents."

The Gestapo asked her full name, age, birthplace. Of course, she'd memorized everything, as had Ilza. Another officer approached. "If they don't speak German," he said, "then they must be Polish. All Jews know German."

The crowd agreed, saying that the girls did not actually look Jewish.

The older lady now felt ashamed. Renia slapped her again. "Find her name and address," Renia told the Gestapo. "Maybe one day I can get back at her."

The Gestapo men laughed. "You're both Polish pigs," one said.

As Renia and Ilza turned away, the child said, "You should have broken her teeth for suspecting you were Jewish."

"She has gray hair, she's elderly," Renia said. "I wouldn't want to disrespect her."

The following morning, Renia woke up early and went to meet Bolk at a designated location. She waited an hour—then two—but he never showed up. It wasn't safe to wait any longer, so she left devastated.

She tried to come up with another plan without success. After several days of staying at the home of a sympathetic German woman, there was a knock at the door. She was shocked to see her sister Sarah, standing in front of her! Renia's joy was overwhelming. It felt like a dream.

Sarah told the story of her escape: She dressed up as a non-Jew and bribed a guard to let her sneak out. She was looking for a place to hide several of her comrades, who she had promised to help get out. Knowing there was no time to spare, Sarah returned to the camp to try to rescue the others.

Renia had to get Ilza settled in Warsaw. After that, she would have to figure out where to settle herself.

Renia bought two tickets to travel to Warsaw with Ilza. They both had fake documents from the same dealer in Warsaw, so the girls sat in different cars.

A little after midnight, the train stopped at the border crossing. Ilza was at the front of the train, so they would check her documents first. Renia waited, nervous but secure that the approach had worked in the past.

No one came. Why was it taking so long? Finally, the door to her car opened. Renia handed over her passport and papers, just as she'd done countless times before.

The guards examined her documents. "This is the same one as in the previous car," one of them said.

Renia's heart raced. She pretended that she didn't speak German.

They did not give her her papers back. They told her, in German, to take her belongings and follow them.

She pretended not to understand.

A polite man translated for her.

She looked right into the guards' eyes. At that moment, a new thought passed through her mind: this is the end.

Without being noticed, Renia opened her bag, pulled out a slip of paper with addresses on it, shoved it into her mouth, and swallowed. She tossed aside her stash of money. Additional fingerprinted documents and a few more Warsaw addresses were sewn into her clothing, but there was no way for her to get them out.

They took her to the customs house, where Ilza was sitting.

The guards asked Renia if she knew Ilza.

"No."

Ilza looked panicked.

The guards took Renia into a small examination room where a German policewoman questioned her. The woman slit open the seams in Renia's clothes and found the hidden documents.

"Please," Renia said.

Nothing.

Renia removed her watch and offered it, on condition that she destroyed the papers.

"No."

The policewoman took Renia to a large hall and reported Renia's attempts to bribe her. She presented the papers and the addresses.

Officers gathered around and laughed. Who are these girls? What should be done to them?

They questioned Renia and Ilza one at a time: Where did you get the papers? How much did you pay? Are you Jewish?

"I'm Catholic," Renia said. "The papers are authentic. I got them from the company where I work as a clerk." Renia stuck to her story. "I intended to visit a relative who works in Germany, but I met a woman who told me that my relative had moved, so I'm returning to Warsaw. I stayed in the country with people I didn't know. I paid them for my stay."

"So let's go back," an officer said. "Show us where you stayed."

"It was my first time in the area." Renia didn't miss a beat. "I don't know the people. My memory isn't good enough to remember the name of the town and the exact house. If I knew, I'd write the address down for you right now."

Renia's answers angered the officer. One of them hit and kicked her, then grabbed her hair and dragged her across the floor. He ordered her to stop lying and tell the truth.

"More than ten Jews with these exact papers were shot to death like dogs just this week," said one officer.

They told her she'd be better off if she were honest. "We never fail to get the truth when we want it."

Renia held firm.

The interrogation lasted three hours, then the officers made her wash the floors and clean all night.

Renia looked around for a way to escape, but everything was bolted tight.

At seven a.m., Renia was thrown into a narrow cell. She'd never been locked up before. Cold and shivering, Renia fell asleep for a minute while sitting on the floor. She woke up when two guards unlocked the cell. She recognized one of them; he used to check her passport at the border. What wonderful luck! He patted her head and told her not to worry. "No harm will be done to you, hold your head up, you'll be out in no time."

If he had any idea I was a Jew, Renia thought, *he wouldn't be so nice.*

The men left and she could hear them arguing in the hall. "No, we can't assume she's Jewish," said the man she had recognized. "She crossed the border with me many times. Just this week I inspected her papers en route from Warsaw to Będzin. We should release her right away."

The older, stricter officer who'd beaten her the night before was not having it. "You didn't know that her papers are fake," he said. "Now we know that Warsaw papers with this stamp are frauds."

Several hours later, a guard showed up at the cell door with Ilza and ordered them to go to the main hall. One of the officers kept Renia's gold watch and other jewelry.

The girls were tied together and taken to the train station, where they were locked in a prisoner car. A German police officer slapped them and didn't allow them to sit the entire way.

Ilza—just seventeen years old—was shaking, terrified. "Do not confess that you are Jewish, ever," Renia warned. "And do not say a word about me."

They disembarked the train, and after thirty minutes of walking, arrived at a large building, decorated with German flags and swastikas. It was the office of the Gestapo.

When they entered the building, they could hear the sounds of people being tortured. They were taken into a room and ordered to stand facing the wall. Renia and Ilza were beaten. "This is the Katowice prison," one of the guards said. "Here, they'll cut you into pieces if you don't tell the truth."

The girls were taken to the damp basement and locked in different cells. Renia curled into a ball, trying to stay warm. Late that afternoon, they were moved to the main prison. The small windows were covered in thick metal bars. The iron gate opened with a loud screech. They were locked in another cell.

At about eight p.m., they were given small slices of dark bread and coffee. Renia and Ilza hadn't eaten for an entire day, but they wouldn't touch the meal. The pitcher was disgusting, the bread inedible.

Escape was impossible. The girls huddled together and discussed options for suicide. Ilza was sure that she would break under torture, that she would tell the Nazis everything. Renia knew that Ilza was young and inexperienced. She explained to Ilza that if she spoke, it would result in many more casualties. "Yes, we failed," she said firmly. "But there's no point bringing suffering to others."

Weary, they lay down on the dirty straw mattresses, but fleas started biting them. They scratched uncontrollably, then they lay down on the bare ground.

In the morning, Renia and Ilza were covered in red dots left by the insects, which were now crawling all over their clothes.

The women were separated and moved to new cells. Renia was given a job "plucking feathers," removing the hard quills from the down. Renia noticed Ilza working nearby, but they couldn't speak. Supervisors with whips stood over them, and talking was not allowed.

Every fifteen minutes or so, a prisoner was called for questioning. A wave of panic washed over her every time the door opened. And then it was her turn.

"Wanda Widuchovska!" the guard yelled.

Renia froze. A whip hit her back.

"Come with me," the guard said.

TWENTY-FOUR

The Cuckoo

August 1943

Renia had no choice but to do what she was told. As she stood, Renia glanced toward Ilza, who was still plucking feathers. Ilza looked up, sympathetic and afraid.

A guard took Renia up several flights of stairs to the supervisor's office. "Go get dressed," he ordered. She put on her skirt and sweater. "For now her name is Widuchovska, but in the interrogation she'll sing and we'll find out her real name," the Gestapo agent said to the supervisor. (Ironically, Renia's last name—Kukiełka—means cuckoo, a songbird that is solitary and secretive.)

Again, Renia walked down the street in chains, led by a Gestapo agent. "Take a good look at the dress you're wearing," he said to her in German, which she pretended not to understand. "After the beating it will be torn to shreds."

Renia didn't feel fear. It was as if he were talking about someone else. She was distancing herself from her body, preparing for what was to come.

Back at the Gestapo building, Renia was asked if she understood German. She said no. In response, she was slapped twice. Renia stood calmly, as if nothing had happened.

Four more Gestapo men entered, along with a female interpreter. The cross-examination began. Renia was drowned in questions. She stuck to her story: The papers were authentic. Her father was a Polish officer taken prisoner by the Russians. Her mother was dead. One of the Gestapo men took out a bundle of papers from a drawer, saying that all the people with these papers were caught at the border. The documents were identical and had the same stamp as the one on Renia's papers.

"Those people's papers may be fake, but it doesn't prove that mine are," Renia said. "The company I work for is real. I've been there for three years. My passage document was written by a clerk from the firm. The stamp is from the mayor of Warsaw. My papers aren't forged."

Annoyed, the Gestapo pushed on. "Everyone who was caught said the same thing, and they were later found to be Jews. They were all shot the next day. If you admit your crime we'll ensure that you stay alive."

Renia smiled. "I have many talents, but lying is not one of them. My papers are authentic, so I can't say they're fake," she said. "I'm Catholic, so I can't say I'm Jewish."

They beat her. The interpreter said Renia was not Jewish, explaining that her features were Polish and her language was perfect.

"Then you're a spy," the Gestapo head said. Everyone agreed.

They asked more questions. After hours of interrogation, she had told them nothing. The Gestapo men were furious.

The chief ordered that Renia be moved to a different room. She was followed by several Gestapo men holding thick whips. They beat her until she passed out.

When she woke up, they started questioning her again. Why wouldn't she confess?

A pistol in his hand, one Gestapo man said, "If you don't want to talk, come with me. I'll shoot you like a dog."

Renia followed him down the stairs. She actually looked forward to it. She could not stand the suffering any longer.

Outside in the street, the Gestapo man asked her with genuine wonder, "Don't you feel it's a waste to die so young? How can you be so stupid? Why won't you just tell the truth?"

Without thinking, Renia responded. "As long as there are people like you in the world, I don't want to live. I told you the truth, and you're trying to force a lie out of me. I will not lie! I'm content with being shot."

He kicked her a few times, then took her back inside and handed her over to the others. Again, she was beaten until she lost consciousness.

The interrogators thought she was dead. When they found she still had a heartbeat, they laid her on a bench.

They called a taxi, and a Gestapo guard took her to another prison, this time in Mysłowice (Miss-lo-VEET-za).

Renia was not the only Jewish courier to be imprisoned, interrogated, and tortured as a Christian Pole. Freedom comrade Bela Hazan also maintained her non-Jewish disguise after the Nazis had found the incriminating holiday party photograph and captured her. It was a burden to maintain secrecy, but her treatment would have been worse if the Nazis knew she was Jewish.

When Bela arrived at Pawiak prison, she longed to see her dear friend and comrade Lonka, who she knew was there too. But Bela was placed in an isolation chamber—a pitch-black dungeon—where she spent most of her time pacing her tiny dank space, nibbling on bread crusts, sipping water and fake coffee, and listening to other prisoners' screams. She was terrified that she would die and no one would know what happened to her.

After six weeks, Bela was moved to the sick ward. She was nearly blind from spending so much time in darkness and was given sunglasses to get used to the light gradually. Then she was moved to a cell.

Inside the cell, she found Lonka, skeletal and pale. For several minutes, they stared at each other, tears filling their eyes. Bela went over to her friend. "I think I know you from somewhere," she said in Polish.

Lonka nodded.

Later, when those around them were distracted, Lonka asked, "Were you caught as a Jew or a Pole?"

"A Pole," Bela said.

Lonka breathed in relief. "How did you end up here?"

"I came looking for you."

"Is it not enough that I'm suffering? Why should you suffer too?" Lonka lay down on her mattress and cried.

"Why are you crying?" their Polish cellmates asked.

"My teeth hurt," Lonka said.

Bela and Lonka were rarely able to speak. They were aware of collaborators and spies who were watching and listening. They tried to work near each other in the yard and chatted on the way to and from the bathroom.

Lonka was beloved in the cell for her upbeat demeanor. But she suffered from stomach pain, and she was not strong.

Their cells were not far from those for Jewish political prisoners. Lonka recognized one of the prisoners, sixteen-year-old Shoshana Gjedna, a Freedom comrade who participated in underground activities in the ghetto. She had been caught carrying a movement newspaper. Shoshana once saw Bela and Lonka in the bathroom, and she urged them to be witnesses of these atrocities after she died.

Once, Bela and Lonka found Shoshana crying in the bathroom while she was cleaning the toilets. When they asked her what was wrong, Shoshana said that the night before she and a group of other Jews had been taken outside and attacked by dogs. Shoshana lifted her dress and showed them a deep bite on her right leg. Bela got medical help and covered Shoshana's injury with a scarf.

Bela worked in the laundry; Lonka peeled potatoes in the kitchen. The work gave them something to do, and they could sneak some potatoes for the Jewish girls.

In November 1942, fifty names—including Bela and Lonka—were called. It was a deportation. The girls didn't know where they were being taken, but Bela was happy: maybe she would finally be able to escape. They were forced onto trains, and many hours later they arrived—at Auschwitz.

Auschwitz-Birkenau was originally established as a prison and slave labor camp for Polish leaders and intellectuals. Bela and Lonka were in a group that was separated from the Jews. They found it difficult to hide their true identity from their people.

Their hair was cut short, and they were each given a striped gown, jacket, and clogs that didn't fit. On their right arms they were tattooed with numbers—how they would be known instead of their names.

At three a.m. there was a roll call. With their bare feet sinking into mud, tens of thousands of women stood for hours in the rain, rubbing their hands and pounding one another on the back to stay warm.

Eventually, they were taken to a barrack. Bela slept on the top bunk, away from the rats, with six other women. She lay in her wet clothes without blankets.

Bela and Lonka were assigned to work in the fields. They were given pickaxes, and they worked from seven a.m. to four p.m. without stopping. Bela's arms ached, but she kept going.

Bela and Lonka wanted jobs that were easier and indoors, where they weren't exposed to rain and cold. They approached their commander and explained that Lonka spoke many languages and Bela was a trained nurse. Lonka was transferred to the office as a translator, and Bela to the hospital ward.

The women's hospital was split into Polish, German, and Jewish sections. Bela was sent to the German division. Three patients lay in each bed, most with typhus, dysentery, and diarrhea. There was no medicine.

As the only Pole, Bela was treated badly by the Germans, who threw their soiled sheets at her head. She had to carry carts of water from the kitchen. Once she was told to bring lunch for the entire staff. She lifted the tray but was simply too weak and dropped it. She was kicked repeatedly in the stomach while lying on the floor. She asked to go back to work outside.

The barracks became more crowded. Typhus, carried by lice, was everywhere, and Bela caught it. When her fever rose above 104 degrees Fahrenheit, she was allowed to go to the infirmary.

There were six women to a bed; Bela had to sit up because there was no room to lie down.

When Bela saw Lonka, who came to visit her, she could see that her friend was also sick. Physically and emotionally, Lonka was losing the will to live. As Bela got better, Lonka got worse. Lonka was brought into the same hospital block, and they were put into the same bed. They held each other day and night.

After six weeks, Bela recovered. She knew she needed to work or else she would be killed. She also needed to stay close to Lonka and nurse her back to health. So Bela began to work at the hospital, and she was given the hardest jobs.

Lonka had typhus, then mumps and dysentery. When Bela heard that the Nazis were going to select which patients should live or die, Bela carried Lonka out of the hospital and back to her own block. She told people Lonka was just worn-out from the grueling work. After the weakest patients were removed, Bela brought Lonka back to the hospital.

Bela worried that nothing could be done. Lonka called Bela over to her bed. "I'm worried I'll leave you alone and you will not be able to keep your secret," she whispered. "You must not reveal that you are Jewish." After spending a bit more time together, Lonka grabbed Bela's hand. "I have pulled the thread of life until its end, but you must go on and tell our story," Lonka said. "See it through. Stay sweet. Look everyone in the eye. Do not lose yourself, and you will survive."

Lonka whispered goodbye, and she died.

Bela could not move. She refused to let go of Lonka's hand. How would she continue to live without her? Lonka had been the only person in the universe who knew who she was, and now she was gone.

Polish women came over, praying and laying holy cards and icons of Jesus in Lonka's hands. Bela hated seeing her best friend die as a Christian, but she did not say anything.

The workers who collected dead bodies approached, but Bela would not let them take her friend this way. She begged a doctor to let her borrow a stretcher, claiming that Lonka was her relative and she wanted to take her to the "cemetery" (where they piled corpses before cremation). He gave his permission.

The Poles who knew Lonka from the prison gathered. Bela removed the body from the bed, cautiously lifting the blanket so the prayer cards and Christian icons would fall to the floor. Four women carried the stretcher, while the others sang mourning tunes. Before saying her last goodbye, Bela lifted the cloth that covered Lonka's face and said a silent Kaddish, the Jewish mourner's prayer.

Bela was alone.

TWENTY-FIVE

"Sisters, Revenge!"

September 1943

Renia was taken to a prison in the town of Mysłowice. She entered a large courtyard in the darkness as attack dogs jumped at her from all sides.

She was locked in a downstairs cell with one bed. She was in unbearable pain from the torture, but she eventually managed to stretch out on her stomach. Her bones, ribs, and spine felt like they'd been broken to pieces. Her whole body was swollen. She could not move her arms or legs.

"I never would have thought any human being could endure such beatings," Renia later wrote. "A tree would have broken like a matchstick if it had been struck like I was, and still I'm alive, breathing and thinking."

A week later, she was taken to an office and questioned by a Gestapo agent. Renia was surprised that she had not been executed.

Then she was led to a room to bathe. She could not undress by herself, but there was a woman in the room who helped her.

Renia saw the results of the beatings. Her body was swollen and bruised. The bath attendant sobbed for her. The woman's concern brought Renia to tears: Could someone still care about her?

The woman told her that she had been imprisoned for two and a half years, one year at Mysłowice. She had been a teacher before the war and had been suspected of political activity. She offered to help Renia get what she needed.

Renia was taken to another cell, one wall lined with bunk beds. The prisoners surrounded Renia and asked questions. Where was she from? Why had she been arrested? What was going on in the outside world?

A young girl, maybe ten years old, carefully watched Renia from the sidelines. Only later did she approach her and ask, "Are there any Jews left in Będzin?" The girl, Mirka, was Jewish. She and her sister had jumped off the train after they had been deported. Her sister was badly wounded. She hadn't known what to do, so she went to the nearby police station for help, but they handed her over to the Gestapo. Her sister was supposed to have been taken to a hospital, but she never heard from her. Mirka had been imprisoned for three weeks. "Maybe the war will end soon," she said. "Every night I dream about the prison gate opening and becoming free again."

"The war will end soon," Renia said. "You'll see, you'll be free one day."

Mirka made sure Renia always got a bowl of food and a straw pillow at night.

The ward held sixty-five women. Each day, some arrived and some left, for interrogations, beatings, or transfers to other prisons or to their deaths.

The supervisor was a cruel woman, always ready to attack a prisoner. One prisoner told Renia that before the war, this woman and her husband had had a little toy shop and sold their goods at markets and fairs. Her husband had died of hunger, so the woman claimed her part-German heritage and joined their side. "You are Polish pigs," she would yell while hitting them. The Gestapo liked her style.

Renia woke up every day at six a.m. The women went to the bathroom in groups of ten, bathing in the sink in cold water. At seven a.m., they stood in rows of three for inspection. They received fifty grams of bread, sometimes a little jam, and a cup of black, bitter coffee.

In the cell, silence. No one dared utter a word. Guards patrolled the hallway.

At lunch, Renia received a bowl of watery broth with some

boiled cabbage and cauliflower leaves. Insects floated on top. No one had spoons.

Dinner was delivered at seven p.m.: a hundred grams of bread with margarine and black coffee. They devoured the bread and sipped the coffee. When they went to bed at nine p.m., the pangs of hunger that ripped through her insides made it hard to fall asleep.

At night, the women were sometimes awakened by the sound of gunshots—probably someone in the men's ward trying to break out. Guards surrounded the building and changed every two hours.

Some mornings, Renia heard stories of prisoners who hung themselves or were beaten trying to run from the bathroom.

Renia spent sleepless nights thinking of escaping. But how?

Every few days, more Jewish women arrived. When a group of twenty Jewish women were assembled, they were sent to Auschwitz. Renia's heart broke every time she saw a group leave. These were her people, even though they didn't know. They held on to the hope that the war would end, right up until the time they had to leave. They wept—all the women wept—when they were forced to go, knowing they were going to die.

Most of the prisoners at Mysłowice were suspected of political activity. Many Polish men and women were executed for helping Jews. Some inmates were criminals—women arrested for selling goods on the black market or on the streets or for turning on the light without covering the window.

Why, Renia wondered, was she still at Mysłowice? Why hadn't she been taken away? Why was she still alive?

Finally, a male supervisor entered the cell and asked Renia what she was in for. She told him that she was arrested while crossing the border. "Let's go."

She didn't know how—a bullet? Hanging? Torture? Or Auschwitz?—but Renia did assume that her end was near.

Auschwitz was only a bus ride away from Mysłowice. Despite the infamous conditions, there were attempts at resistance inside the camp. At Auschwitz, the underground included youth from different countries and philosophies.

Anna Heilman first heard about the resistance from one of her block mates, a Jewish girl who had passed as Polish. Fourteen-year-old Anna had arrived at Auschwitz a year earlier with her older sister, Esther. They were from an upper-middle-class Warsaw family, and they grew up with nannies and visits to gourmet ice cream parlors. They now worked as forced labor at the Union Factory, which made detonators for artillery shells for the German army.

When she heard about a rebellion, Anna was eager to join. Although she was young, she had been part of The Young Guard in the Warsaw ghetto. She'd seen the ghetto uprising; she craved more rebellious activity. The Polish underground was planning to attack the camp from the outside, while the inmates would attack from the inside.

In preparation, Anna and her comrades collected matches, gasoline, and heavy objects, and placed them in predetermined locations. About five women in each block participated, coordinated by one leader.

On Anna's way to work each day, she'd pass a man who worked as a locksmith and who always smiled at her. One morning, she felt brave and spontaneously asked him for a pair of insulated wire-cutting shears (to break through the electrified barbed wires). He looked at her, stunned, and said nothing.

For days, she worried that she had trusted the wrong person. Then, one afternoon, he put a box on her worktable at the factory. The other girls teased her, saying he liked her. Anna slipped the box under her table and peeked inside. It contained a whole loaf of bread! Thankfully, there was no inspection that day, so she smuggled the bread back to camp, hidden under her clothes. Anna showed her sister the bread, and they noticed that it had been hollowed out. Inside they found shears with red insulated handles. The sisters hid this treasure in their mattress.

The group had no weapons, but Anna worked in a factory with gunpowder. She asked her sister, Esther, one of the few women who was stationed in the powder room, to steal some. It would not be easy. The entire factory was open, and the tables were surrounded by surveillance paths. The women were not allowed to stop their work to eat, drink, or use the bathroom. The room measured only ten by six feet.

Esther agreed to steal the gunpowder. She worked twelve-hour shifts in front of a machine, pressing the gray powder into pieces the size of checkers.

Anna walked down the dusty hall, past several supervisors, and headed to the gunpowder room as if she were on trash collection duty. Esther's spot was near the door. She handed Anna a small metal box, the kind used for garbage. Esther had hidden bits of gunpowder, wrapped in knotted cloth, in the garbage. Anna brought the box to her table, took out the cloth packets, and slid them under her dress. In the bathroom she divided the packets with several other women before heading back to camp. If ever there was an inspection, the girls tugged open the cloth and dumped the powder on the ground, rubbing it in with their feet.

In all, there were about thirty Jewish women who smuggled gunpowder. In one day, three girls could collect about two teaspoons of powder.

They gave the powder to the men, who were allowed in the women's camp to remove corpses. A Russian prisoner made the dynamite into bombs using empty sardine or shoe polish cans as casings.

One day, without warning, the plans changed. A group of workers who were organizing the revolt found out that they were going to be killed. The attack would happen now or never.

On October 7, 1944, the Jewish underground attacked a Nazi with hammers, axes, and stones, and then they blew up a crematorium. They dug out some weapons they had hidden and used them to kill several more guards, then they cut through the barbed wire and ran.

The Nazis shot all three hundred of those who tried to escape.

Afterward, the Nazis found the handmade grenades and traced the gunpowder back to the gunpowder room. They began an investigation, torturing people until they confessed.

Esther was taken to a punishment cell. Anna was horrified, grief-stricken. Later, Anna was also taken in for questioning. She was beaten, then the interrogation began: "Who stole the gunpowder? Why?"

Anna said nothing.

"Esther confessed everything," her Nazi interrogator said. "So you may as well tell us."

"How can Esther confess to anything?" Anna asked. "She is innocent and she is not a liar."

Esther was bruised and battered when they released her. Anna took care of her.

A few days later, the Nazis came back for Esther and three other girls who worked at the factory. They were sentenced to hanging.

Anna was inconsolable. She was held in the hospital to prevent her from killing herself. She tried desperately to contact her sister, to see her one last time, but she couldn't.

Before she died, Esther wrote a last letter to her sister. She also wrote to her friend Marta, asking her to "take care of my sister [Anna] so that I may die easier."

"Camp sisters" were family.

The four Jewish women were hanged in a public ceremony intended to scare the other prisoners and stop further rebellion. All Jewish women prisoners were forced to watch. They were beaten if their eyes strayed for a second. Anna's friends hid her and would not let her watch.

In her last breath, before the noose tightened, one of the women cried out: "Sisters, revenge!"

TWENTY-SIX

The Light of Days

October 1943

Outside Renia's cell at Mysłowice, a guard was waiting. Renia was stalling, sure she was going to her death.

"Any day, someone is going to take you out for a new task," the guard said. "You'll be working in the police kitchen."

What? She wasn't going to Auschwitz or to an interrogation?

Instead, Renia had an assignment outside the prison, at the police station. Her shift ran from four a.m. to four p.m. She left her cell in darkness that gradually became dawn and then daylight. The cook gave Renia food, and over time she regained her strength. She couldn't bring food back to her cell, but she did give her prison dinners to women hungrier than she was.

One of the guards who accompanied Renia to work treated her graciously, giving her cigarettes, apples, and buttered bread. "I can't tell why I trusted him," Renia later wrote. "I genuinely felt that he was honest and that his friendship could benefit me."

One evening, when the prisoners were asleep, Renia wrote a letter to her Freedom comrades. She had to take a chance. She asked the friendly guard to mail it to "her parents in Warsaw." She explained that since she'd been arrested, no one knew where she was. He promised he'd attach a stamp and send it.

After the fact, Renia worried. What had she done? What if the guard gave it to the Gestapo? The letter was written in code, but it contained information and addresses. She wanted her comrades to know she was alive and to know where she was. As the days passed, it seemed less and less likely that anyone would ever find her.

Late one night, four women and a baby were brought into Renia's cell. They were Jewish, except for one woman, Tatiana Kuprienko, a Russian born in Poland. Tatiana explained that she had been sheltering and feeding six Jewish adults and a baby. She arranged for them to get Polish papers, hoping they could find work in Germany. One of the women left for Germany and wrote to say she found a job.

"Two and a half months later, the police arrived at my house with a seventeen-year-old Polish boy," Tatiana said. "The boy told the police that I was hiding Jews. We were all arrested."

At the police station, Tatiana was beaten. The Gestapo told her she was lucky to be Russian, otherwise she'd have been hanged.

Two days later, the Jewish women and their husbands were transported to Auschwitz. Two days after that, the Jewish woman who had gone to Germany was brought in and beaten. She didn't reveal the name of the counterfeiter or say that she knew Tatiana. They were both brutally tortured.

Tatiana told Renia that she thought that one day she'd be free. "I have a wealthy brother-in-law in Warsaw, maybe he'll bail me out," she said.

Renia smiled, assuming she had gone insane from all the beating.

A few days later, Tatiana's name was called. She was taken by the Gestapo, but a few minutes later, she returned laughing. She was free! She was going home!

When she came over to kiss Renia, she whispered in her ear that her brother-in-law paid half a kilogram of gold for her, an amount that today would be worth $25,000.

Renia was thrilled. If it was possible to bribe the Gestapo, maybe there was hope.

Bribery wasn't the only way out. One afternoon, a taxi arrived at the camp gate. Two men in civilian clothes got out, presented papers saying they were undercover Gestapo men, and headed to the men's ward. The plainclothed Gestapo called out the names of two young men who'd been convicted of leading a partisan group. They told the guards to unchain the men, then they took them to the waiting car.

As soon as they left, the guards contacted the Gestapo headquarters. It turned out that they were fake Gestapo agents, and two prisoners had just escaped.

Renia was delighted. "That incident awoke my passion for life and my faith in freedom," she later wrote. "Who knows, maybe a miracle could happen to me, too."

The prison directors were furious. Discipline was tightened, and cases were reopened. One morning, Renia was told she was no longer going to work at the police kitchen. Instead, she was hit in the head and locked in a dark cell. She was now suspected of being a spy.

Renia was moved to a cell for female political prisoners. She lost all hope of getting out.

She overheard from another prisoner that Ilza had confessed to being Jewish and was hanged. Her heart broke into a million pieces, but she didn't twitch a muscle.

Day and night, Renia thought about the fate of her comrades. Her memories were fading. She couldn't concentrate or remember her testimony. She wasn't sure that she could trust herself if they decided to interrogate her again. Her head hurt all the time, and she was so weak she could barely stand. She thought about Ilza's young face.

She had been so close to freedom.

TWENTY-SEVEN

The Great Escape

November 1943

"This is for you," a woman whispered, handing Renia a note while they were waiting in the bathroom. "It was given to me while working in the field."

Renia was startled.

"The woman is coming tomorrow to get an answer," she said.

Renia's hands shook as she took the paper. She didn't open it until that night, when everyone around her was asleep. The first thing she noticed was the handwriting; it looked like Sarah's! She wrote that many comrades were still alive. They had found places to hide in Poles' homes. She said that she had learned of Renia's fate from the letter that Zivia received in Warsaw. The guard had actually mailed it! Now Sarah and the others wanted to know how they could help. They would do anything to get her out.

Renia reread the note dozens of times.

It was past midnight, but she checked to make sure that everyone was still asleep. She slipped out of bed and snuck over to the monitor's desk and found a pencil. Sarah, always prepared, had included a piece of paper for her reply.

Renia wrote: "First, you must pay the woman who carried the note generously, since she risked her life. Second, would it be possible to pay her to trade places with me, so I could go out to the field? Then we can meet and decide what to do."

In the morning, in the bathroom, Renia slipped the note to the woman Belitkova, who had passed Sarah's letter to her. They arranged to meet again that night.

All day, Renia rejoiced in the news that Sarah and her friends were safe.

That evening, another note arrived. "Everything will be ok," it said. "After much persuasion, Belitkova agreed to let you go to the field in her place. She'll be paid with valuables and plenty of money. I'll send the goods to her house today."

The next day, Renia changed into Belitkova's dress and the two women switched places for roll call. It was a cold November morning, so Renia wrapped her face in all the rags she could find. None of the guards recognized her.

Renia arrived at the worksite with Belitkova's group. They began carrying bricks and loading them onto a train car. Renia was weak and barely able to do the work. She kept looking for Sarah.

Finally, in the distance, Renia saw two well-dressed, elegant ladies, one of them with her sister's confident gait. She saw Sarah looking around. *She probably doesn't recognize me*, Renia thought.

Renia walked toward the gate. The female prisoners watched, puzzled. "They're acquaintances of a cellmate," Renia lied.

The chief guard followed Renia. He didn't know who she was or know that she was a political prisoner. When the sisters met, they could not hold back their tears. Sarah handed the guard pastries, and he allowed the visit.

The woman with Sarah, Halina, had been sent from Warsaw by Zivia. "It doesn't matter if you fail," Halina said. "You must try to get out. Your life is in danger anyways."

They arranged to meet at that same spot the following week. The girls would bring clothes for Renia to change into so she could disguise herself and escape.

The visit didn't last long, but Renia felt renewed. She repeated Halina's words in her mind: *You must try.*

As soon as Renia returned from work, she collapsed. Her head throbbed, and she could not stand up. She had a fever of 104 degrees for three days. She worried she would miss her chance, but she could not move.

Renia's fever finally broke, but she fainted again. She spent two more days in bed. She had to get well so she could see her sister. *You must try.*

Finally, on November 12, 1943, Renia was ready to return to the fields.

"No," the cell monitor said. "You can't go to the fields today."

"Why not?" Renia asked, panicking. "You let me go last week." Belitkova had agreed once again to swap places, for a large sum.

"It's too risky," the woman said. "What if the camp chief realizes you are from the political prisoners' cell? We'll all be in trouble."

"Please," Renia said. She had nothing left to offer. "Please, I beg you."

Eventually, the cell monitor changed her mind and let her go. A miracle.

Again the supervisor didn't recognize her. She was held upright by women on her right and left so she didn't collapse while marching to the square. There were fifteen women and five guards. Renia began lifting bricks while searching for Sarah and Halina. Where were they?

Finally, at about ten a.m. she saw them approaching. Renia slipped away, but a guard spotted her. "How dare you leave work without my permission!" he yelled.

Sarah flirted with him, trying to get him to look the other way.

"Come back at two p.m. with cigarettes and liquor," Renia said to Halina.

The workers were angry with Renia for disobeying the head guard. She was putting everyone at risk. Renia went back to work.

A few hours later, a guard called her over. "So, you're a political prisoner," he said, to her horror. "You're very young and I feel sorry for you. Otherwise, I would have informed the camp commander." He told her not to think about trying to escape. They would cut her into pieces.

"There's no chance I'd escape," Renia said. "I'm smart enough to know that I'd be caught. I was arrested for stealing across the border; I'll probably be released soon. Why would I spoil my chances?"

Renia assumed that the women had told the head guard her secret. No wonder: if Renia escaped, they'd all suffer.

Now everything was more difficult. Both the guards and her fellow prisoners were watching her.

Where were Sarah and Halina? Had something happened?

Finally, she saw them walking back in their direction.

This time, Renia knew she couldn't sneak away, so she tried another approach. "Come with me, please," she asked the head guard. He followed.

The four of them—three Jewish girls and a Nazi

guard—stood behind the wall of a bombed building. Halina passed the guard several bottles of whiskey. He gulped down an entire flask while they stuffed his pockets with cigarettes. Renia picked up a few small bottles of liquor and packs of cigarettes and distributed them to the guards, then asked them to stop the other women from going behind the wall. The guards weren't too concerned because they knew the head watchman was with her.

At this point, the head guard was drunk. Renia convinced him to go see if the other women were looking in their direction.

He stumbled off.

This was her chance. Now or never.

Renia was not the only Jewish female member of the youth resistance movement to attempt a jailbreak.

After the Kraków bombings, Gusta's husband, Shimshon, was missing. She went to every police station until she found him, then refused to leave his side. She was taken to the Montelupich prison, another Gestapo jail.

Gusta was placed in a cell with fifty women, including several Jewish underground operatives. Gusta organized a daily routine for her fellow prisoners: as long as water was available, she made them wash and brush their hair and clean their table, to maintain hygiene and humanity. She initiated regular discussions of philosophy, history, literature, and the Bible. They wrote and recited poetry. When a member of the group was taken out to be shot, those who remained expressed their grief in song.

Gusta wrote her memoirs between beatings, using scraps of toilet paper sewn together with thread from the girls' skirts. She wrote the story of the Kraków resistance with the other women's help. Everyone was given a fake name for security, in case the work fell into the wrong hands. Gusta only included events that were already known to the Gestapo. She wrote until her hand became too tired, then other cell mates would take turns writing with the pencil that had been smuggled into the cell. To muffle her voice as she dictated the words, the other women would sing and watch for the guard. The women made four copies of the diary. Three were hidden in the cell—in the stove, the door upholstery, and under the floorboards—and one was smuggled out by Jewish auto mechanics. After the war, text scraps that had been hidden under the cell floor were found.

On April 29, 1943, Gusta and her comrades knew that they would be on the next transport to death and decided this was their moment. While they were being led outside to the transport truck on a crowded city street, several of the women stopped and refused to move. The Gestapo guards were confused. One took out his gun. One of the women ran behind him and pushed his arm up into the air.

The girls took a chance and ran. The Gestapo shot at them in the crowded streets as they searched for cover. Only Gusta and another woman survived.

Gusta did not know it, but her husband also broke out of jail that day. He and Gusta met up in a small town outside Kraków where several resistance members were hiding.

They resumed the fight: organizing fighting troops, writing and distributing underground bulletins, and engaging in combat. A few months later, the couple was arrested. This time, they were both killed.

Renia's heart was pounding. When the drunk guard turned away, the women seized the moment. Sarah and Halina helped Renia put on a new dress, shawl, and shoes. Then they walked away, Sarah and Renia in one direction, Halina the other.

The sisters began to run as fast as they could. When they came to a hill, Renia did not have the strength to climb it. An Italian prisoner was on the same route. He held out his hand and helped Renia to the top.

Renia barely made it over the barbed wire fence surrounding the square. Eventually, the girls landed in the street. Renia's dress was caked in mud from climbing, but she continued to run.

A car approached. "They got us!" Sarah cried. "We're doomed."

But the car drove on.

They ran.

With every passing minute, Renia became weaker. She tried

to keep moving, but her legs failed her. She fell. Sarah picked her up. "Renia," Sarah said. "Please keep going. If not, it will be the end for us both. Make the effort. I have no one but you. I can't lose you. Please."

Renia stood and moved on. Her legs felt gummy, and they buckled under her.

People on the street stared at them as if they were insane. They were wearing muddy rags, and their shoes were covered in dirt. They looked suspicious.

They had walked four miles. Sarah wiped Renia's face and tried to make them both look presentable. She knew a German woman who lived nearby. Only four more miles to go.

Renia walked slowly. They saw a group of guards in the distance. It was too late for them to turn around.

They kept going. The men looked them over, then walked on.

Renia was so tired she had to rest every two or three steps.

"There's not far left to go," Sarah said.

At last they approached the town. Renia's vision was blurry, and she was covered with sweat. Renia stopped at a well in someone's yard and splashed water on her face.

The sisters walked through the town, Renia using all her strength to stay upright. Sarah guided them to a two-story building, then she picked up her tiny sister and carried Renia up the stairs like a bride. "I don't know where she found the strength," Renia later wrote. The door opened, but before Renia could even see the inside, she fainted.

When she came to, she changed clothes and got into a clean bed. Her teeth chattered even under the blankets as spasms of cold shook her.

Sarah told the German lady of the house that Renia was a friend of hers who was ill and needed to rest. She was told that Renia could not stay there long.

That night, Renia and Sarah walked two and half miles to another village. At about eleven p.m., they arrived at the house of Polish peasants, where they were greeted warmly. They'd heard of Renia and were full of praise for Sarah's skills. They offered Renia food, then sent her into a bunker. Renia and Sarah slipped underneath the stairs and climbed down a ladder.

Twenty comrades greeted Renia with joy, "as if I was just born."

Renia had to rest, but Sarah told them the tale of her escape. Renia looked at the faces in the bunker. She was burning with fever, and she still felt like she was being chased. Would that feeling ever end?

A few hours later, Halina arrived and told them about her escape. "As I started walking away from you, I turned my jacket inside-out and took off my kerchief," she said. "Ahead of me, I saw a railroad worker. I asked him if he cared to join me as we walked. He took one look at me and said 'happily.'" She held his arm as they strolled. A few minutes later, two guards ran toward them on their way to the camp. They asked if she'd seen three women escaping. They said they had not and kept walking. The worker escorted her to the tram, unaware that he was helping a fugitive!

The following morning, Halina went to Warsaw without a problem. She was safe.

For days Renia rested in the bunker, which had been built to house two or three people and was overcrowded. People slept together on a few beds. Food was prepared by the Polish family who owned the house. The people in the bunker lived in constant fear of the neighbors finding out. Once she was stronger, Renia was transferred in the middle of the night to another hiding place.

There were still a few hundred Jews held in the Będzin liquidation camp and local ghettos, but the number dropped with each transport. Sarah and other girls with non-Jewish features continued to sneak out and try to save as many people as possible, even though it was increasingly difficult to find places to hide them. Renia was still too weak to go outside.

The young Jews believed that the only way to safety was through Slovakia, where—at least for the time being—Jews had relative freedom. But it was difficult to make the necessary connections. And after their betrayal by Socha, the group was particularly cautious. They didn't know who to trust. Many Polish families who housed Jews were getting nervous and asking them to move on. They needed a new way out.

Renia and the group stayed in constant contact with Warsaw. Zivia and the other Freedom leadership urged them to go to Slovakia, though they also offered to bring Renia to Warsaw, where it might be safer. But Renia didn't want to separate from her comrades. "Their fate is mine," she said.

At last the leadership found trustworthy smugglers. They planned to send one group first, then the rest in waves. The initial group left in early December, dressed as Poles and equipped with fake travel documents and work papers. The others stayed in the bunkers.

A week later, the smuggler returned. The mission had been a success! This time, their comrades did write, telling them that the journey was less difficult than they'd anticipated. "Do not," they warned, "wait any longer."

On December 20, Renia and the others waited all day to find out who would go in the second group. At midnight, a comrade arrived.

"Get ready for the journey," she told Renia. Eight people would leave in the morning.

Renia refused.

Sarah was on a mission, and Renia hadn't seen her in two weeks. "She's my sister," Renia said. "She risked her life during my camp escape. I can't go without her consent." She certainly couldn't leave without saying goodbye.

But the Gestapo was after Renia. "Wanted" posters showing her face, calling her a spy, and offering a cash reward, hung on the streets. She needed to leave right away. The leaders promised that Sarah would be in the next group.

Renia finally agreed.

The train left at six a.m. Renia styled her hair in a different way and wore new clothes to make her less recognizable. She took nothing but the clothes on her back.

At the station they met their guide, as well as the other six people who would flee with them, including Chajka Klinger, who had escaped from the liquidation camp by bribing a guard.

Despite passing several guards and Gestapo men on the way, Renia and the others made it to the train. For Renia, who risked being recognized in this area, this was the most dangerous leg of the entire journey. Fortunately, no one asked to see their papers or inspected their bags.

Eventually they made it to the small village near the border. They rested for a few hours, then began the final part of their trip, which was on foot.

They left as a group—six Jews, two smugglers, two guides—heading toward the snow-covered mountains in the distance. The first few miles were flat. Renia wore only a dress—no jacket—but she didn't feel the cold. When they reached the mountains, walking became more difficult. The snow was knee-deep, and they sometimes slipped and slid.

The guides knew the route well. They climbed toward the peak—6,233 feet, more than a mile elevation. Despite the cold, their sweaty clothes clung to their skin.

In the distance, they saw border patrol agents. They lay down, covering themselves in the snow, until they passed.

Renia was still weak from prison, and she had trouble breathing in the altitude. The smugglers encouraged her, and she pushed on.

Slowly, quietly, they passed the border patrol building and approached the summit. They stumbled on each step, sinking into the snow. They were almost there.

Finally, after six hours of torturous hiking, they found themselves in Slovakia!

Renia had left Poland.

Now she could share her story with the rest of the world.

TWENTY-EIGHT

The Arrival

December 1943

Slovakia, a state formed just before World War II, was no Jewish paradise. The ruler of the country was antisemitic. Most of the nation's Jews had been deported to Polish death camps in 1942. After that, there was a break in the deportations that lasted until August 1944. During those two years, Jews lived in relative security, either pretending to be Christian, or because they were able to pay bribes.

Resistance leader Gisi Fleischmann deserves some credit for this period of relative calm. She joined the Zionist party, took on several public leadership roles, and in 1938, she ran an agency that aided German Jewish refugees. International money passed through a Swiss account to her.

At the beginning of the war, Gisi tried—unsuccessfully—to arrange for large-scale Jewish immigration to Palestine. In wartime, Gisi maintained contact with numerous international leaders, telling them what was going on.

Slovakia had promised to send its people to German work camps, but the Slovak government struck a deal with the Nazis, asking them to deport their Jews instead. Slovakia was the only European country that paid the Nazis to take their Jewish citizens. Gisi negotiated with Germans and the Slovak government, eventually collecting funds and offering bribes to the Nazis to reduce the number of Jewish deportees. She set up work camps for Jews in Slovakia to save them from being taken to Poland. She was also instrumental in collecting international funds to help smuggle in Jews, known as "hikers," on an underground railroad from Poland, like the one Renia had taken.

In this new country, Renia and her hiker comrades descended the mountain into a valley. In the distance, they saw a bonfire. The comrades stopped at the spot where they were supposed to meet their local guides and started their own fire.

Their feet were wet and in danger of freezing. They dried their shoes and socks in the blaze as they rested for about an hour. The original guides returned to the Polish border to bring over more groups. The comrades then put on their shoes and walked with the Slovaks toward a small village.

They went to a stable with horses, cows, pigs, and chickens. It was warm inside, and the hikers rested on bales of hay and fell into a deep sleep.

At noon the next day, the landlady, dressed in traditional mountain garb—a kerchief and colorful dress with felt shoes—brought the comrades lunch. She asked them to stay put because the villagers were on their way to church, and she didn't want them to be seen.

Renia went back to sleep. Many of the others shared stories about what they had been through. Their journey wasn't over, and neither was the war. At night, a sleigh arrived and the comrades rode to the next village. A few hours later, they reached a town and were placed in a single room and told not to leave until their car arrived. There was plenty of food here, as long as one had the money to buy it, and fortunately the comrades each had a bit of cash. They ate and slept more.

That night, a car waited for them on the outskirts of the village. As they drove, the driver asked them questions about the Jews in Poland. He was heartbroken to learn that many were the sole survivors of their families. He was horrified to hear stories of German atrocities.

The driver took them to Mikuláš, a town with a Jewish community that would take care of them. Renia was in awe of how well planned the whole operation was, everything arranged to the smallest detail. In Mikuláš, the car stopped at the community center. The driver fetched a Jewish person, who took them to an inn. There, they met Freedom comrade Max Fischer, who reported that the rest of the first group was already in Hungary, waiting to go to Palestine. Suddenly, Renia felt like a bird released from a cage, finally able to untuck her wings.

The Mikuláš Jews were nervous about police raids. The comrades were housed in a school auditorium set up for refugees. As far as the police were concerned, the shelter housed only people who had been caught by border patrol and were waiting for the authorities to look into their cases. The large room had beds, a table, a long bench, and a heater. Food was available for purchase from a special kitchen set up by refugees themselves. The comrades were to wait here for a few days until the next group arrived.

The next day, Benito, a member of Slovakia's Young Guard, arrived, asking about the surviving comrades. Benito warned Renia not to get too relaxed because a huge number of Slovakian Jews had been deported to Poland. Here, too, Jews were required to wear a patch to identify them.

Each day, Jews arrived in the shelter from Kraków, Warsaw, and other cities and villages. Many were chatty and energized, but they still whispered out of habit. Renia learned about communities across Poland, as well as the ghettos and labor camps that still existed.

During this time, Chajka and Benito fell for each other. Benito was the same age and had been a longtime Young Guard leader. He had survived the Slovakian deportations by escaping to Hungary, after arranging for sixty of his comrades to escape, too. He was connected with movement leaders in Europe and Palestine. Chajka had lived through the horrors he'd only heard of secondhand. She stayed up late, telling him her stories, warmed by the auditorium's large oven.

Benito wanted to protect Chajka. "She talked for hours and hours, as if fearing that she would not have time to deliver all of the information," he said. He sat with her and held her hand "to feel the person who is carrying all of this on their heart and soul."

A few days later, the next group of comrades from Poland arrived. But Sarah was not with them.

The Jews planned to go to the Hungarian border together, accompanied by a bribed policeman. Their cover story: the comrades were Hungarian nationals and the policeman was taking them to the border to deport them. Renia and Chajka stayed behind, waiting for Sarah and Benito.

The next week another group arrived. Still no Sarah.

Then Renia got a message. She and Chajka were to leave immediately because they had received papers to immigrate to Palestine! This was Renia's dream.

Renia wrote to Sarah, encouraging her to hurry.

On the day Renia was to leave, the group received a letter from a smuggler. The snow in the mountains was now hip-deep along the Poland-Slovakia border. It was impassable, so there would be no more crossing.

Sarah would not be coming.

Renia sensed she would not see her sister again.

She was the last remaining Kukiełka.

In early January 1944, with both a heavy heart and hope, Renia and several comrades left for Hungary. They took the train to the final station in Slovakia and disembarked. They were going to cross the border hidden in a freight train. The engineer climbed down from the locomotive and gestured for them to follow him. They climbed aboard and crouched inside with several other escapees. The engineers, paid per person, crammed them into hidden corners, and the train began to move. Everyone prayed they would not be searched at the border. The heat was intense, and Renia found it hard to breathe. Fortunately, the ride did not take long.

At the first station inside Hungary, the engineer released a long wave of steam, creating a heavy cloud. "Go!" he yelled. The smoke hid the escapees as they dashed for the station. The engineer bought them tickets and showed them where to catch a passenger train to Budapest.

The ride took a day and a half. The comrades stayed quiet, trying to avoid notice. "The Hungarians themselves have semitic features," Renia wrote. "It's hard to tell who's Jewish." Most Jews spoke Hungarian, not Yiddish or Hebrew. Jews were not required to wear ribbons or stars on their sleeves. There were no document checks or inspections on the train.

The Budapest train station was crowded and hectic. The police inspected passengers' bags. Renia passed through quickly and hurried to the address they'd been given.

They took the tram to the Palestine Bureau, which was bustling, echoing with German, Polish, Yiddish, and Hungarian pleas. Everyone wanted papers, everyone laid their claims as to why they needed to leave right away. The British, however, maintained their quotas and limited Jewish immigration. First in line for visas were the Polish refugees who'd endured the most terrible tortures. That meant Renia.

Renia waited impatiently for her departure date, which kept being postponed. First, her photos had not been received. Then, when the passports were ready, the visas were delayed from Turkey. The closer she was, the more nerve-racking the wait. The uncertainty was constant. "The situation in Hungary is good for now, but it could change at any moment," she said.

Renia needed the correct papers to go to Palestine or to legally stay in Hungary. She watched as people were regularly stopped in the streets for inspections; those not registered with the police were arrested. Jews who had felt safe, now felt on edge.

Renia went to the Polish consulate, to report herself as a refugee from Poland. The Polish captain lobbed endless questions. One of the clerks asked: "Is Madame really Catholic?" Renia insisted she was.

"Thank God," he said. "Until now only Jews disguised as Poles have come to us."

Renia pretended to be outraged. "What?" she asked. "Jews disguised as Poles?"

"Yes, unfortunately," he answered. Her performance was never ending.

Renia expected to get her papers in a few days, but a month later, she was still waiting. During that time, Renia began to write her memoir. She knew she needed to tell the world what had happened to her people, her family, her comrades, but it was hard for her to find the words with which to express the horrors she'd experienced. She scribbled in Polish, using initials instead of names, figuring out for herself what had happened and what it meant.

Renia and her comrades had never been to their spiritual homeland, but they thought Palestine would feel familiar. "They will receive us with open arms," Renia wrote, "like a mother receiving her children." They yearned to see the land where their suffering would be in the past and they would be free of constant fear.

Still, Renia worried. "Will our friends in Palestine understand what we'd gone through?" she asked. "Will we be able to live a normal life, a life like theirs?"

Eventually, it was Renia's turn to go. Despite her longing and her relief, she could not feel happiness. "The memory of the millions that were murdered, the memory of the comrades who . . . have fallen before reaching their destination, doesn't let up," she wrote. She would be okay one minute, and then out of nowhere, the image of Jews being shoved into a train car would flash through her mind, sending shivers through her body. Her family, her sister—she couldn't allow herself to think about those who were no longer with her.

Renia traveled through Romania, Bulgaria, Turkey. As she left Europe, she imagined a future where she could look at people and not fear their stare.

Benito and another comrade met Renia and the other escapees at the Istanbul train station. Jews roamed freely through the streets. Renia marveled at how strange this was, not to be hunted. When she resumed travel, she crossed Syria before finally reaching her destination.

On March 6, 1944, Renia Kukiełka, a nineteen-year-old Jewish girl from Jędrzejów, arrived in Haifa, Palestine.

PART FOUR

The Emotional Legacy

Interviewer: How are you?
Renia: [Pause] Usually, I'm fine.
　　　　—Renia Kukiełka, Yad Vashem testimony, 2002

"We had been liberated from the fear of death, but we were not free from the fear of life."
　　　　—Hadassah Rosensaft, a Jewish dentist who stole food, clothing, and medication for patients at Auschwitz

TWENTY-NINE

Fear of Life

March 1944

Renia made it. She had left Poland a fugitive, wanted by the Gestapo, and she was now in her dreamland. She spent some time recovering, and then she settled on a kibbutz in Galilee. She said she felt comfort, "as if I'd arrived at the home of my parents."

Many survivors came to Palestine to live and work on kibbutzim. Still, there were difficulties. Renia remained tormented by memories of those she had lost. "We feel like we're smaller and weaker than the people around us," she wrote, describing how she and other survivors felt shortly after arriving. "Like we don't have the same right to life as they do."

Like many survivors, Renia did not always feel understood. She traveled throughout Palestine, giving talks about her experience in the war. Sometimes she felt that the people she was addressing didn't understand—or didn't care.

There are many reasons why the stories of Jewish women in the resistance were lost over time. The majority of fighters and couriers were killed, so they did not live to tell their tales. In other cases, female narratives were silenced for both political and personal reasons.

The politics of Israel in its early years influenced how Holocaust stories were told. Soon after the end of the war, Israeli politicians tried to create a split between European and Israeli Jews. European Jews, the Israelis said, were physically weak and passive, compared to Israeli Jews, who saw themselves as the strong next wave. Israel was the future; Europe—even if it had been the cradle of Jewish civilization for more than a thousand years—was the past. The stories of the tough resistance fighters didn't fit the stereotypes they were trying to create.

A decade after the war, people were ready to hear about the concentration camps and trauma. In the 1970s, tales of individual rebels were replaced by stories of everyday resistance.

The history in the United States is different. Some say that American Jews did not discuss the Holocaust in the 1940s and 1950s because of feelings of fear and guilt, or because they were trying to fit in with their middle-class non-Jewish neighbors. But this isn't true. In fact, there was a great deal of writing and discussion about the Holocaust in the postwar years. American Jews struggled with how to talk about the genocide, not whether they should. By the 1980s, so many Holocaust books were published that earlier tales—like Renia's and the courier girls'—were drowned out.

Today, many writers fear that glorifying resisters places too much focus on personal power, implying that survival was more than luck, judging those who did not take up arms, ultimately blaming the victim. They worry about propelling the myth that Jews had more control over their situations than most of them did and avoid telling the story.

And then there is gender. Women are routinely dropped from stories in which they played key roles. They are too often erased from history. In the youth movement, women were usually the ones directed to escape and share the truth; they were to be the firsthand historians. And they did their job: Many of the earliest records of the resistance were written by women. But as the authors of these accounts, the women reported on the activities of other people, usually men, rather than their own. The major histories were then written by men, who focused on the work done by men, not the courier girls.

When women tried to tell their stories, they were often deliberately silenced or censored. Some were accused of making it all up. Some women were blamed by relatives for leaving their families to fight. Women felt judged by those who believed that pure souls died and the sneaky ones survived. When women encountered these negative messages, they often stopped sharing the truth of their experiences.

Of course, some women silenced themselves because remembering was just too painful. They felt their role was to give birth to a new generation of Jews and to keep their pasts to themselves so they could create a "normal" life for their children. Many survivors were young women in their twenties, and they wanted to move forward with their lives. They did not want to become "professional survivors."

Freedom itself was also difficult. In addition to experiencing horrible trauma, these young women had lost their homes, their families, and their childhoods. They had not had the chance to study or train for a career, and they had no social networks. They did not know where to go, what to do, who to be, or how to love or trust.

Faye Schulman, who spent years wandering the forest on partisan sabotage missions, described liberation as "the lowest point in my life." After the war, she wrote: "Never in my life had I felt so lonely, so sad; never had I felt such yearning for the parents, family and friends whom I would never see again." She was alone in the world and felt her life had no purpose or direction.

After the war, Faye became a government photographer.

She tracked down her surviving brothers and met a man who would become her husband. "We felt an urgency to proceed quickly with whatever love was left in us," Faye wrote. She and her husband moved to Canada and raised a family. For decades Faye spoke publicly about her war experience. "Sometimes [the] bygone world feels almost more real to me than the present," she wrote. A part of her always remained rooted in her lost universe.

Survivors also felt guilt.

In the summer of 1944, from the window of her hiding place in Warsaw, Zivia could see weary horses pulling farmers' carts full of Germans fleeing for their lives. It was time for the Polish resistance to rise up.

Zivia put word out through the Polish underground press that all Jews should fight alongside them for an independent, strong, and just Poland. The Warsaw uprising began on August 1, and Jews—including women—joined the fight.

Zivia and twenty-two comrades insisted on active combat. It meant everything to her that the Jewish Fighting Organization remained alive and engaged.

The Polish underground had expected to fight for a few days, but the battle lasted two months. Warsaw was destroyed, turned into a heap of rubble three stories high. Eventually, the Poles surrendered. The Jews—especially those who looked traditionally Jewish—once again had to escape through the sewage canals. This time, Zivia was exhausted and nearly drowned.

Zivia and the other Jews went into hiding, but they were nearly discovered several times. At one point, the Germans began digging trenches on their street, almost revealing the bunker where Zivia was hiding. A rescue group from the Polish Red Cross arrived just before they would have been found. Couriers had contacted a Polish doctor at a nearby hospital, and he'd sent a team to retrieve them. The two most Jewish-looking comrades had their faces bandaged so they wouldn't be seen and were carried out on stretchers. The healthiest put on Red Cross armbands and pretended to be among the rescuers.

When the Russians finally liberated Warsaw, thirty-year-old Zivia felt empty. She described the day when the Soviet tanks rolled in. "A mob of people exuberantly rushed out to greet them in the town market place," she wrote. "The people rejoiced and embraced their liberators. We stood by crushed and dejected, lone remnants of our people." This was the saddest day of Zivia's life: the world she'd known officially ceased to exist.

Approximately three hundred thousand Polish Jews remained alive, 10 percent of the prewar population. These included survivors of camps, "passers," people in hiding, fighters in the forests, and—the majority—the two hundred thousand Jews who had lived out the war in Soviet territory. These Jews had nothing.

Zivia returned to Warsaw to work with survivors, setting up

safe communes and attracting Jews to Freedom. As always, she was the mother figure who everyone looked up to, yet she kept her own feelings private. In 1945, Zivia asked the movement to move her to Palestine. She didn't find life easy there, either. She lived on a kibbutz, but she did not think survivors were adequately welcomed. She felt depressed and guilty. She was supposed to have died.

Zivia was sent on a speaking tour, which she called "a circus." She received invitations from countless groups, and she felt she could not turn any down. In June 1946, six thousand people gathered to hear Zivia deliver an eloquent, eight-hour testimony in Hebrew, spoken without notes. The audience was riveted. She talked about the war, the movement, and the Jewish Fighting Organization, but never about her feelings or personal life. These speeches ripped open wounds that she so wanted to close.

The following year, Zivia was selected for a major role at the international World Zionist Congress. She and Antek met up in Switzerland, where they were secretly married by a rabbi. She returned to Israel pregnant. Antek followed a few months later. Despite the heroic reputation of this power couple—they were the last remaining Zionists of the Warsaw ghetto uprising command—Antek worked in the fields, Zivia in the chicken coop. Zivia shunned the public eye. According to those close to her, she did not think of herself as special, just as someone who did what had to be done.

Zivia and Antek decided to found their own kibbutz to memorialize the past. Some in the movement feared that this kibbutz would focus on the traumas of yesterday. After some struggle, they established the Ghetto Fighters' House, made up mostly of survivors. Zivia relied on work and motherhood—a constant balancing act—to forget her past and forge forward.

Many of the people on the kibbutz suffered from post-traumatic stress disorder and night terrors. Many feared that "catastrophe could hit with no notice." They were afraid of thunder and lightning (which reminded them of bombings). Despite these fears, they worked hard to become a productive entity, just as they had been trained.

Zivia remained principled, restrained, and driven by movement ideals. She had two children. Like most survivors, Zivia and Antek were overprotective and nurturing parents who didn't talk to their children about the war; their children knew not to ask. Many children of survivors felt pressure in their own right. Once they were old enough to understand what their parents had gone through, the children did not want to cause any problems, and they felt the need to act happy and be hardworking.

Throughout her life, Zivia felt guilty, worrying that she could have saved more, done more, done things earlier. She could never let go of the question: Why did I survive? She also never let go of her cigarette habit. She died of lung cancer in 1978.

Antek was also haunted by the past. He didn't want to live in a world without his wife. He died two years after Zivia, in a taxi on the way to a ceremony in her honor.

Life was hard for Polish resistance fighters in postwar Poland, too. Poland was governed by the Soviets for decades. Anyone who had supported the Polish underground during the war could have been considered a Polish nationalist or a rebel. Poles who helped Jews often hid their heroic actions for fear they'd be accused of being on the wrong side of the state. One Polish woman who had sheltered a family that moved to Israel had to ask them to stop sending thank-you gifts with Israeli flags because the presents made the neighbors suspicious.

Some Jews gave themselves new identities. Halina, who helped Renia escape from prison, was actually Irena Gelblum. After the war, she and her boyfriend went to Palestine, but she didn't like it. She moved to Italy, changed her name to Irena Conti, and became a poet. Later, she returned to Poland, again changing her identity and friends, and her past became a deeper and deeper secret.

For some, survival itself was too painful. Chajka Klinger made it to Palestine, but she could not overcome her depression. She and Benito moved to a Young Guard kibbutz, where they took part in the communal life. Chajka spoke at assemblies and conferences. The Young Guard published passages from her diaries, but her words had been edited to change their meaning. She was outraged. Her thoughts—for an intellectual like her, her identity—had been tampered with by the very movement for which she had dedicated her life.

Chajka and Benito moved to a new kibbutz, and she began to feel settled. Her happiness made her feel guilty as she started editing her diaries into a book. Then she became pregnant and gave birth to a son. She began to suffer from mental illness and stress, but she felt alone. She did not have a survivor community who understood her.

The head of The Young Guard decided that her husband, who worked in refugee aid, would return to Europe. Chajka had to give up the calm life she had struggled to create. She did not stay in Europe long before returning to Palestine to give birth to her second son. She suffered from severe postpartum depression, unable to get out of bed for weeks and afraid of taking medicine for fear she was being poisoned. She was hospitalized against her will. When she was released, no one discussed what had happened.

Chajka became distant from her friends. She became pregnant again. During this time, her diaries were used without her permission to criticize The Young Guard leadership, placing her in conflict between her own truth and her loyalty to the movement. Again she suffered from postpartum depression and was hospitalized. As part of the treatment, she was forced to talk about the Gestapo torture, which left her feeling traumatized all over again.

Chajka had suicidal thoughts when she was in hiding during the war, and those thoughts never left her permanently. On the fifteenth anniversary of the Warsaw ghetto uprising, forty-two-year-old Chajka Klinger killed herself. She survived the war, but she could not live with the memory.

THIRTY

Forgotten Strength

1945 and Beyond

Renia continued to speak out and share her story. One day, some couriers in a displaced persons camp in Cyprus mentioned her name. In front of them, a man fainted.

He was Renia's brother.

Zvi Kukiełka had escaped to Russia and joined the Red Army. After the war, he ended up at a refugee camp, but he had assumed Renia had been killed. Their younger brother Aaron was also alive, having survived the work camps because of his blond good looks, charm, and melodic voice, singing in a church choir. In time, both brothers would make their way to Palestine.

Renia harbored hope that Sarah had somehow been able to escape. But after she arrived in Palestine, she found out that Sarah had been caught near the Slovakian border, along with a group of comrades and orphans. "Please take care of my sister Renia," was her last recorded request. She did not survive.

In 1945, Renia completed her memoirs in Polish. Hakibbutz Hameuchad, an organization that published many survivor stories, had her work translated into Hebrew and published it the same year. Excerpts of Renia's story were translated into Yiddish and included in *Women in the Ghettos*. In 1947, the full book was retitled *Escape from the Pit* and published in English. Renia also contributed to an anthology about Frumka and Hantze. Renia found writing therapeutic. After she told her story, she felt able to move on.

The English book was lost over time. It may have been due to the flood of American Holocaust publishing, or the 1950s "trauma fatigue" experienced by many Jews, who felt weary hearing about the horrors of the war. The story may also have become less popular because Renia was still alive. Renia did not promote her writing. For her, the point of publication was to put Poland behind her.

Renia remained close to her brothers and her former comrades. She learned Hebrew, participated in social activities, and worked on the kibbutz. She met Akiva Herscovitch, a man from Jędrzejów who had moved to Palestine in 1939, before the war. Renia had been friendly with his sister back in Poland.

Akiva remembered Renia as a young, attractive teenager. They quickly fell in love, and in 1949 they married.

Akiva did not want to live on a kibbutz, so Renia moved with him to Haifa, Israel's principal port city. She worked at the Jewish Agency, receiving immigrants from ships, until two days before her first child was born, in 1950. Five years later, she gave birth to her daughter, Leah, named for her mother.

Renia had prayed for a daughter, feeling that naming her child after her mother was the only way she could ever honor her memory. Many survivors' children speak of feeling like replacements for dead relatives, especially grandparents they never knew. Missing relations had an impact on survivor families. Family members took on unusual roles because many families were left without grandparents, aunts, uncles, or cousins.

When her children were young, Renia stayed at home. She was funny, full of life, and a good judge of character. She maintained her sharp appearance, collecting dozens of skirt suits, each to be worn with specific shoes, handbags, and accessories.

Renia went to work as an assistant at a preschool when her kids were older. After that, she was an administrator at a health care clinic. Akiva was the manager of a national marble company and then an electric company. He was also an artist who created mosaics and woodcuts that hung at local synagogues. Although he grew up in a religious family, Akiva no longer believed in God. Most of his large family had been murdered. He refused to speak a word of Polish, and he only used Yiddish if he didn't want his children to understand what he was saying. The family spoke Hebrew at home.

Although Renia gave talks about the war, stayed in touch with Freedom comrades, and spent hours talking about the past with her brother Zvi, she rarely spoke about the Holocaust with her immediate family. She wanted to show her children joy and to encourage them to explore the world. Their lives were filled with books, lectures, concerts, classical music, home-baked cookies, travel, and optimism. She loved lipsticks and earrings. On Friday nights, their house was crowded with fifty people dancing as records played. "Life is short," she said, "enjoy everything, appreciate everything."

Despite their joyous home, Renia's children always felt the darkness of the past. They sensed that they were absorbing Renia's history, even though they did not quite comprehend it. Leah read her mother's memoir when she was thirteen, but she didn't understand most of it. As an adult, Renia's son, Yakov, changed his last name from Herscovitch to the Israeli "Harel" in order to distance himself from the old land. He didn't read his mother's book for the first time until he was forty.

Renia was a combination of strong and fragile. She was asked to testify at an important Nazi trial, but Akiva wouldn't let her. He worried that the experience would be too stressful. Renia never asked for financial compensation from Germany because she didn't want to have to tell her story—she didn't owe them anything, even her narrative. On Holocaust Remembrance

Day, the family turned off the television. Everyone worried that Renia's memories would be too difficult for her to face, that she might crack.

When she was in her sixties, Renia read her own book in disbelief. How had she possibly done those things? All she recalled from that period was her confidence and an incredible desire for revenge. Her adult life was so different—happy, passionate, and filled with beauty.

Renia spoke to her brothers on the phone every morning. Many survivors maintained strong bonds with those who shared their experience, visiting them across continents and gathering for annual commemorative events. "Sisters" from camps, ghettos, and forests became surrogate families, the only people they had left from their early lives.

Other survivors put the war behind them and kept their memories to themselves. "I raised my children and immersed myself in daily life. I tried to contain my personal story," Bela Hazan wrote after the war. "I didn't want my children to grow up in the shadow of the Holocaust." But of course her story remained "alive inside of me with the same strength."

On January 18, 1945, Bela was working in the Auschwitz infirmary. When the Russians neared the camp, she was one of thousands sent on a Death March to Germany. In rags and without shoes, she walked through the snow for three days and nights with no food or water. Thousands died on the way. The

Nazis assumed Bela was not Jewish, so they sent her to another camp, where she continued to work in the infirmary before escaping. She was liberated by Americans. Her 1945 memoir opens with the chapter "From Death March—to Life."

The Americans helped her reach the Zionist office in Paris, where she finally gave up her Polish identity as Bronisława Limanowska. She no longer had to pretend she was someone she was not. She went to Italy with a group of Jewish Brigade soldiers from Palestine. Bela spent three months in Italy working as a counselor, guiding and listening to the harrowing tales of forty-three young girl survivors aged six to fourteen. The group was called "The Frumka Group" after Frumka Płotnicka, who was posthumously awarded a Polish Order of the Cross.

In 1945, Bela immigrated to Palestine, where she married and raised two children. Despite her Freedom background, she never felt connected with the underground fighters. She kept her story to herself, but never forgot it. At one point she was contacted by a former comrade, who gave her a copy of the incriminating Gestapo Christmas party photograph of Bela with Lonka and Tema. She placed this heirloom next to her bed, where it stood for the rest of her life.

In 1990, Bela was approached about publishing her forty-five-year-old memoir. At first she refused, afraid to face her horrific memories. Then, on further reflection, she decided to tell her story for the sake of the innocent and brave who did not live. For Lonka.

Bela was modest, never thinking of herself as a hero. If anything, she felt guilty that she hadn't saved her family. Throughout her life, Bela continued to work for the less fortunate, dedicating her life to helping the poor and sick. She remained an optimist, always hopeful, always grateful.

Comrades Vitka and Ruzka stayed together during the war and for most of their lives afterward. They were separated immediately after the end of the war, when Vitka was sent out to check on the condition of Jewish refugees in Poland, while Ruzka was sent to Romania to meet with leaders from Palestine. The journey was difficult. Postwar, the region was torn up and dangerous, and Ruzka felt both free and yet still anxious walking on the streets.

Ruzka was then sent to Palestine. She had always dreamed of going to the Zionist homeland, but now she felt as if she didn't know where she belonged. When she landed at a camp for illegal Jewish immigrants, she was appalled by the terrible conditions. No one came to receive her, and she felt forgotten. When word of her arrival got out, leaders and their wives began to visit her, but it made her feel like a curiosity rather than part of a community. Eventually, she was sent on a speaking tour to share her experiences as a fighter.

None of this was easy for Ruzka. She joined a kibbutz and began writing her memoirs, but was desperately lonely. She felt that most people didn't understand her. She wrote to Vitka, urging her to join her, but Vitka was still in Europe supporting refugees. Vitka and comrade Abba became a couple, and they worked on an underground railroad, shepherding Jews by foot.

Abba was still focused on revenge. He and Vitka gathered Jewish fighters and became leaders of a new brigade of Avengers. Based out of Italy, they deployed fighters across Europe. Abba was captured and imprisoned in Cairo. Vitka continued the work. The group poisoned bread that was sent to a Nazi camp near Nuremberg. Thousands of Nazi prisoners became sick.

The Avengers moved their operation to Palestine. Vitka arrived in Palestine and settled on the same kibbutz as Ruzka. Despite that brief postwar split, Ruzka and Vitka spent most of their adult lives entwined, their children growing up together.

Ruzka and Vitka worked in the fields, and Ruzka became an educator and kibbutz secretary. With time, they developed additional careers. Ruzka and Abba founded a Young Guard center for the study of the Holocaust and the resistance.

In 1988, less than a year after Abba passed, Ruzka died of cancer.

Unlike Abba and Ruzka, Vitka never talked about her past. Vitka defied the odds again and again. When her first child was three, Vitka developed tuberculosis. Her doctor told her she had four months to live; she told him, "I will live."

She did. She was put in isolation, unable to see her son up close for nearly two years. While recuperating, she enrolled in correspondence courses in history, English, and French. Though she was told it would be dangerous to have another child, she had a daughter several years later. On the kibbutz, Vitka helped with children's education.

At age forty-five, she went to university and trained as a clinical psychologist, completing a BA and advanced degrees. She developed a successful and busy practice treating children and retired at eighty-five.

After the war, Vladka Meed settled in New York with her husband, Benjamin. They helped establish Holocaust survivor organizations, memorials, and museums, including the United States Holocaust Memorial Museum in Washington, D.C. She died in 2012, a few weeks before her ninety-first birthday. Hela Schüpper settled in Israel and died at ninety-six, leaving behind three children and ten grandchildren. Anna Heilman became a social worker at the Children's Aid Society in Canada, where she lobbied the government about humanitarian crises.

Even as an old woman, Renia remained vital. "When she walked into a room," her son said, "it was like a fire hit." Her own family did not know how she could maintain her joyful demeanor and optimistic outlook. "How could someone have gone through what she went through be so happy?" her granddaughter asked.

Renia's husband, Akiva, died in 1995, and until her late

eighties, Renia was being wooed by new suitors. She and her friends moved into a senior home. She continued to be funny, quick, and center stage, hypnotizing people with her looks and energy. While she liked the attention, Renia never accepted the advances of her would-be beaus. In her twenty years as a widow, she did not have one boyfriend. Her dedication to her husband was a model of loyalty for her children and grandchildren. "Family is the most important thing," she often said. "Always stay together."

Renia's grandchildren and great-grandchild were her utmost treasures. She told them her stories, passing on as much of her heritage as she could. Like many survivors, she found it easier to open up to her grandchildren. Many had learned to overcome their fear of intimacy; they were no longer as afraid of losing those they cared about. Renia took her grandkids to the Ghetto Fighters' House on Holocaust Remembrance Day, recognizing how important it was to send her story into the future. Like many of the third generation, her grandchildren—who had learned about the Holocaust in school and had an intellectual and proud response to it, too—asked her many questions, which she gladly answered.

On Monday, August 4, 2014, nearly ninety years after she was born in Jędrzejów, Renia died. She was buried at the Neve David cemetery in Haifa, next to Akiva, exactly where she wanted to be. She had outlived most of her friends, but her funeral was filled with seventy loving people from her old-age home and the health clinic where she once worked, as well as many of her children's friends who loved and respected her, too. She was also surrounded by the strong family that she had cultivated from nothing, the new branches of a damaged family tree. One of her grandsons gave a eulogy, remembering her sparkling conversation and her sense of humor. He knew the stories of her past, and now he could share them with future generations. He summed up his grandmother's life—Renia's life—saying, "You always fought like a real hero."

EPILOGUE

In the spring of 2018, more than a decade after I first found *Women in the Ghettos* in the British Library, I got on a flight to Israel. Those women had lived in my head for years, but now I was preparing to meet with their actual children so I could discover another piece of the story.

In Israel, the most nerve-wracking and exciting meeting I had was with Renia's son and daughter. I had visited online archives and tracked down a "Renia Kokelka" whose details matched the excerpts. I found her Hebrew memoir. I discovered a genealogical report, which included the mention of a son, and I was able to track him down.

Before I met Renia's family, I traveled the country and visited the National Library, where the 1940s books of obituaries and literary essays that had been the source material for *Women in the Ghettos* were located. I went to the Ghetto Fighters' House, a museum with a bunker reconstruction, and a small gallery that housed an exhibition on women in the resistance. I met scholars, curators, archivists, and the children and grandchildren of many of the women remembered in these pages.

I had already visited Holocaust museums and archives in North America and interviewed many other children of survivors, but the Israeli families felt different. Their world was more political, more live-wire, charged with strong feelings and high stakes. I often met with the "Holocaust spokesperson" of the family, the relative who most passionately studied the subject. I was grilled by one who was worried that my interest was superficial. Another was concerned that I would steal the work her group had accomplished. Yet another did not want to tell me much unless I agreed to write a movie with him.

Of all the meetings that week, it was the encounter with Renia's children that I was most nervous about. I felt I had a writerly bond with her. What would I do if her family disliked me or refused to tell me anything?

It turned out I was worried for no reason. When I entered their home, I found Renia's son and daughter to be kind and welcoming. They were open with their remembrances about their mother and grateful for the things I knew about Renia that I could share with them. In Renia's daughter, Leah, I recognized features that I had seen in Renia's archival photographs, her strong jawline and intense eyes.

Our conversation deepened my appreciation for Renia. Yes, Renia was funny, sharp, sarcastic, theatrical. But she was also a fashionista who traveled the world. She loved to laugh and cherished her friends. She was a force of joy.

Poland has had a complicated relationship with Jewishness. I took my first trip to Poland soon after I originally discovered *Women in the Ghettos* back in 2007. As part of my research, I met people in their twenties and thirties who recently found out they were Jewish; their grandparents had kept their Jewish heritage hidden during the years of Soviet rule. On the same trip, I had dinner at a Jewish-themed restaurant in Kraków where musicians played songs from *Fiddler on the Roof,* and my fellow diners were busloads of clapping German tourists.

As part of that visit, I met distant relatives of mine who had stayed in Poland after the war and lived through Soviet rule and antisemitic attacks. One of them relayed how as a young boy his parents had grabbed his hand and the three of them had fled from the ghetto into the forest; he survived the war in a partisan camp. He was livid about the "new Jew" culture in Poland, convinced that this was just a way for Poles to make money.

Now, returning to Poland by myself in the summer of 2018 to conduct research for this book, I was unsure what to expect. It became immediately clear that the Poland I had experienced a decade earlier was no longer. Warsaw had become an urban center. I stayed on the forty-first story of a hotel that looked out onto a futuristic cityscape, which had once been the area of the ghetto, and before that, where all my grandparents lived. I walked down the city streets, passed monuments to Frumka Płotnicka and the sewage canal of Zivia's story, to POLIN, the museum of the history of Polish Jews, with exhibits about the Holocaust and the thousand years of rich Jewish life that preceded it. It seemed that Poland needed, wanted, and missed its Jews.

I felt very comfortable in this Poland. On the other hand, the government had just passed a law making it illegal to blame

Poland for any crimes committed in the Holocaust; violators could be put in jail. After decades of Nazi and then Soviet repression, Poland was in a new nationalist phase. They felt their status as victim in World War II was important. The Polish underground was celebrated. The Polish people wanted to be recognized as heroes fighting grand enemies.

Once again, Poland embodied two extremes. I found it deeply troubling that the government was making laws about how history was to be written. But I also understood that the Poles felt misunderstood. Warsaw had been decimated. The Nazi regime enslaved, terrorized, and killed many Christian Poles. (Renia was jailed and tortured as a Pole, not a Jew.) To be held responsible for the war did seem unfair, especially when the Polish government did not collaborate with Nazis. Certainly, this claim was unjust to those who risked their lives to help Jews, a number which could be greater than we know.

Then again, there were many Poles who did nothing, and worse, many who turned on and turned in Jews, selling them to the Gestapo for pennies or a bit of sugar. Many Poles are guilty of blackmailing, profiteering, and stealing Jewish property. I have tried to understand the Polish sentiment of victimhood without playing a game of who suffered more, Poles or Jews.

I think it is important to tell these complex stories. History isn't black and white, good and evil. We must confront the past honestly and face the ways we are both victims and aggressors. Knowing the truth is a necessary step for self-possession and growth.

* * *

On one of my last days in Poland, I planned a pilgrimage to find Renia's birthplace. I felt a bit carsick in the back seat of an old car with no air-conditioning, soaked from a walk in a thunderstorm so I could stand on the site of Frumka's fighter bunker.

As we drove, I imagined how long it must have taken the couriers, in disguise, in 1943 to cover the same route. After a five-and-a-half-hour trip, we arrived in Jędrzejów, my last stop on this journey. I had the address for Renia's childhood home, where her story began in 1924. Klasztorna Street was easy to find, but number 16 did not seem to exist. If we counted plots, marked by trees more than a hundred years old, we ended up at a small stone house.

My Polish-speaking guide went ahead of me to talk to the owner. I didn't understand the words they were saying, but I did understand that the woman was shaking her head no.

"She says the addresses changed," my guide told me. "Number sixteen must have been a wooden house that burned down. She said she never heard of the family. She asked if they were Jews."

"Did you tell her?" I asked.

"I tried to avoid the question," my guide said. "They get scared here," she whispered, "worried that the Jews will return to take back their property."

I was not invited inside.

I took some photos of the outside, then we drove through the area, taking in the setting sun, the fertile fields. This was nothing like the gray-hued Poland of my imagination. In the car, my driver, my guide, and I were three women from very different backgrounds—a Pole, a Lithuanian, and a Jew. We had been brought together by Renia and the other female fighters. We were ready to reclaim these stories and to fight for the truth, all of us feeling strong, proud, and, at least for the moment, safe.

AUTHOR'S NOTE: ON RESEARCH

This was a challenging book to write. My research took me around the world and included sources in several languages. Most of my primary source material comprised memoirs and testimonies. Some were oral histories (both audio and video) and others were written accounts in Hebrew, Yiddish, English, Polish, Russian, and German. Some were translated, some were translations of translations, some I translated myself.

Some accounts were fact-checked, edited, or cowritten with scholars. Others were diaries or raw testimony, filled with fury and passion.

Some were written during or immediately after the war; these sometimes contain mistakes, conflicting details, and omissions—things were simply not known or changed for security reasons . . . or emotional ones. Some were written quickly, in a desperate attempt not to forget.

Like many early scribes, Renia wrote out of a desire to tell the world what happened. She tried to be objective, to avoid her personal opinions. In her writing, she often uses the pronoun "we," and at times it can be hard to discern whether she is referring to herself, her family, her community, or to the Jewish people at large.

Other testimonies were written later, often in the 1990s.

These tellings may have benefitted from insights gained with time and perspective, but memories may also have been altered by the years.

I also sifted through articles, letters, and notebooks, and I interviewed dozens of family members, each of whom had their own—sometimes contradictory—versions of stories.

There were many differences in the dozens of accounts; the details of events were often at odds, and the dates varied. Sometimes the same person offered personal testimonies on several occasions over the years, and their own tellings differed dramatically. Some biographers and historians shared accounts of these women that differed from the women's own stories. Sometimes the differences in primary sources had to do with taking responsibility, with whom to blame.

At times, I merged details from many accounts to build a single, fuller picture, to present the most emotionally authentic and factually accurate story that I could. Whenever I was in doubt, I let the women's testimonies and truths speak for themselves.

A final word on words:

For ease, I have used the term "Pole" to refer to a non-Jewish (Christian) Polish national; Jews were also Polish nationals.

The women in my story refer to the Nazis as "Germans," although there were anti-Nazi Germans as well.

Some scholars object to the term "courier girls." "Courier," they argue, sounds trivial. In fact, these women were weapons smugglers, intelligence scouts, and connectors. "Girls" is also considered to be belittling. While some were teens, most couriers were young women, around age twenty. I wanted to stress their youth; I do not intend to diminish them in any way.

ACKNOWLEDGMENTS

This book would not exist without the support of myriad people. I owe my deepest gratitude:

To Alia Hanna Habib for being the first to see the potential in this project, to Rachel Kahan, for nurturing that potential with wisdom and generosity, and to Alexandra Cooper for her insight and compassion. I could not have dreamed of more intelligent and dedicated guides.

To the team at HarperCollins Children's: Cat SanJuan, Amy Ryan, Erin Fitzsimmons, Allison Weintraub, Mark Rifkin, Audrey Diestelkamp, Emma Meyer, Cindy Hamilton, Kadeen Griffiths, Shona McCarthy, Victoria Abate, Josh Weiss, Jill Amack, Nicole Moulaison, Erin Wallace, Tara Feehan, Patty Rosati, and Laura Raps. To Winifred Conkling, for her acumen and celerity.

To the teams at William Morrow and the Gernert company, for their verve and creativity. To the Hadassah-Brandeis Institute for initially funding the translation of *Freuen in di Ghettos* and believing in the importance of this material from day one.

To all the resistors' relatives who benevolently shared their memories and impressions. To all the scholars who took the time to meet with me and share their knowledge. To the many academics who replied to my emails, directing me toward resources and specialists. To all the librarians, archivists, and photo archivists for their indispensable help. To my smart and dedicated research assistants, translators, and fixers. To my writing mentors. To my children's carers, for making my every workday possible, and even pleasant.

To all those who shared their family stories, sent me links to resistance articles and partisan songs, and listened to me yammer on about Jewish women outsmarting the Gestapo for more than a decade. To all those—and I'm sure there are many—who I forgot to include here due to the vagaries of memory.

To Zelda and Billie, for offering inspiration and hope. To Bram, for arriving at exactly the right time.

To Jon, for everything.

Finally, to Chayele Palevsky, a Vilna partisan who Skyped with me in 2019, and implored me to pass on her message: "We must never let this happen again. Hate is our fiercest enemy. Be peaceful, be loving, and work to create a world of happiness."

GLOSSARY

Antisemitism: Prejudice against Jewish people

Couriers: During World War II, these were women who transported documents, information, money, weapons, supplies, and even people between cities in Poland

Gestapo: The official secret police of Nazi Germany

Ghetto: A closed-off area in a city where Jews were restricted

Holocaust: The mass genocide of the European Jews during World War II

Judenrat: A community-based agency run by Jews that managed and policed Jewish ghettos and communities

Labor Camps: Nazi Germany built and managed concentration camps before and during World War II; labor camps exploited the labor of people held at the camps

Marxism: The belief in a classless society

Nazi: A member of the National Socialist German Workers Party, also known as the Nazi party

Partisan: A member of an armed group formed to fight against an occupying force

Shabbat: The day of rest and worship in the Jewish religion, observed from sunset Friday to Saturday evening

Yiddish: The main Jewish language in Poland before the war

Zionist: A person who believes in the creation of a Jewish homeland in Israel

SOURCE NOTES

Introduction

xix "five major concentration and death camps . . . eighteen forced-labor camps" Nechama Tec, Resistance: Jews and Christians Who Defied the Nazi Terror (New York: Oxford University Press, 2013), 148.

Part 1: Ghetto Girls

xxi "Is someone needed . . . to smuggle in contraband . . ." Emmanuel Ringelblum, *Notes from the Warsaw Ghetto: The Journal of Emmanuel Ringelblum*, trans. Jacob Sloan (New York: ibooks, 2006), 273–274.

Chapter 1: Here, We Stay

6 "Where we live, that's our country." Samuel D. Kassow, "On the Jewish Street, 1918–1939," *POLIN, 1000 Year History of Polish Jews—Catalogue for the Core Exhibition*, eds. Barbara Kirshenblatt-Gimblett and Antony Polonsky (Warsaw: POLIN Museum of the History of Polish Jews, 2014), 248 (description of the Bund's ideals).

Chapter 3: Zivia

21 "badges of shame." Zivia Lubetkin, *In the Days of Destruction and Revolt*, trans. Ishai Tubbin and Debby Garber (Tel Aviv, Isr.: Ghetto Fighters' House, 1981), 18.

Chapter 4: Terror in the Ghetto

25 "A father, brother, sister or mother . . ." Renia Kukiełka, *Underground Wanderings* [in Hebrew] (Ein Harod: Kibbutz Hameuchad, 1945), 17.

26 "The result was that the Germans hardened . . ." Ibid., 218.

26 "If you saw a dead body on the street . . ." John Avnet discussion of his film *Uprising* at the Directors Guild, New York City, April 22, 2018.

26 "One day, the Germans invented a new way to kill Jews," Kukiełka, *Underground Wanderings*, 21.

27 "For them, killing a person was easier . . ." Ibid., 27.

Chapter 5: Education and the Word

31 "With all our strength we tried to give them back . . ." Chana Gelbard, "In the Warsaw Ghetto," Leib Spizman, ed. *Women in the Ghettos* [in Yiddish], (New York: Pioneer Women's Organization, 1946), 8.

33 "strong against the clouds in these stormy times." Ibid., 9–11.

Chapter 6: Becoming the Jewish Fighting Organization

36 "This train is taking you to the worst death camps. . . ." Vera Slymovicz testimony, 23–24, Alex Dworkin Canadian Jewish Archives, Montreal, Canada.

36 "irresponsibly sowing the seeds of despair . . ." Lubetkin, *In the Days*, 92–93.

37 "That's how the life of a Jew . . ." Chajka Klinger, "The Pioneers in Combat," *Women in the Ghettos*, 23–28.

39 "It is better to be shot in the ghetto . . ." Lubetkin, *In the Days*, 112.

40 "We came together and sat . . ." Ibid., 121.

40 "The proposed act is an act of despair . . ." This quotation merges accounts of the speech given in Gutterman. Bella Gutterman, *Fighting for Her People: Zivia Lubetkin, 1914–1978*, trans. Ora Cummings. (Jerusalem, Isr.: Yad Vashem, 2014), 189; Lubetkin, *In the Days*, 122; Yitzhak "Antek" Zuckerman, *A Surplus of Memory: Chronicle of the Warsaw Ghetto Uprising*, trans. Barbara Harshav (Berkeley: University of California Press, 1993), 214.

Chapter 7: On the Run

41 "Your father and I are still young . . ." Kukiełka, *Underground Wanderings*, 38.

42 "Hide still until nightfall," Ibid., 40.

42 "Where is Mother?" Ibid., 42.

44 "No matter what happens . . ." Renia Kukiełka video testimony, Yad Vashem archive #4288059, June 20, 2002.

45 "Escape," . . . "Go wherever you can." This scene is based on a combination of Kukiełka's *Underground Wanderings* and her Yad Vashem testimony.

46 "That's a strange name," Kukiełka video testimony, Yad Vashem archive #4288059, June 20, 2002.

47 "Yes, this is her . . ." Kukiełka, *Underground Wanderings*, 49.

48 "What do you want?" Ibid., 50.

49 "Where can I spend the night?" Kukiełka, *Underground Wanderings*, 52; she gives a different account in her Yad Vashem testimony.

Chapter 8: Heart of Stone

51 "My aunt fell ill . . ." Kukiełka, *Underground Wanderings*, 56.

52 "Is this Miechow?" Ibid., 57.

53 "Sarah," . . . "Would you like it if Renia came to see you?" Ibid., 59.

54 "If we don't survive, then please fight . . ." Ibid., 61.

54 "My heart," . . . "turned to stone." Ibid., 61.

Chapter 9: A New Way Forward

59 "Don't cry," . . . "They are not worth your tears." Klinger, "Girls in the Ghettos," *Women in the Ghettos*, 17–23.

63 "In Grochov, the conditions were much worse . . ." Kukiełka, "The Last Days," *Women in the Ghettos*, 102–106.

64 "There's no help coming . . ." Kukiełka, *Underground Wanderings*, 67.

64 the town of Lubliniec . . . The JTA, or Jewish Telegraphic Agency published the report of this revolt on January 8, 1943; the incident took place on October 4, 1942. The women's revolt is described in both the JTA report and in *Women in the Ghettos*, though with different details in each. JTA.org.

Chapter 10: Fighting Back

66 "I pledge to engage in active resistance . . ." Gusta Davidson Draenge, *Justyna's Narrative*, trans. Roslyn Hirsch and David Hirsch (Amherst: University of Massachusetts Press, 1996), 141.

66 "We want to survive as a generation of avengers . . ." Ibid., 141.

68 "floating office" Ibid., 64–67.

71 "This is the last supper." Ibid., 126.

71 "The war will soon be over," Ibid., 6–7.

Chapter 11: Rebellion

74 "Now the shoes!" Vladka Meed, *On Both Sides of the Wall*, trans. Steven Meed (Washington, DC: United States Holocaust Memorial Museum, 1993), 78.

75 "The Jews are firing at us!" Lubetkin, *In the Days*, 147.

79 "All the hearts are broken . . ." Kukiełka, *Underground Wanderings*, 74.

79 "We've obtained a few passports," based on Ibid., 74–75.

Part 2: Devils or Goddesses

81 "They were not human, perhaps devils or goddesses." Stroop to his cellmate, after the war, cited in Witold Bereś and Krzysztof Burnetko, *Marek Edelman: Being on the Right Side*, trans. William R. Brand (Kraków: Bereś Media, 2016), 170.

Chapter 12: "I'll Go"

86 "barbarian butchering of the Jews," Kukiełka, *Underground Wanderings*, 83.

86 "No excuse, no argument." Ibid., 83.

86 "If you don't hear from us again . . ." Ibid., 85.

87 "Of course," . . . "I'll go." based on Ibid., 88.

88 "From here, it's quiet," Ibid., 88–91.

89 "I'm here to see Zosia," Ibid.

90 "connector." Sheryl Silver Ochayon, "The Female Couriers During the Holocaust," www.yadvashem.org/articles/general/couriers.html.

90 "human radios," Lenore J. Weitzman, "Kashariyot (Couriers) in the Jewish Resistance During the Holocaust," in *The Encyclopedia of Jewish Women*, https://jwa.org/encyclopedia/article/kashariyot-couriers-in-jewish-resistance-during-holocaust.

92 "We couldn't cry for real . . ." Naomi Izhar, *Chasia Bornstein-Bielicka, One of the Few: A Resistance Fighter and Educator, 1939–1947*, trans. Naftali Greenwood (Jerusalem: Yad Vashem, 2009), 237.

Chapter 13: Inside the Gestapo

95 "Can you speak German?" Bela Ya-ari-Hazan, *Bronisława Was My Name* (Tel Aviv, Isr.: Ghetto Fighters' House, 1991), 34–67.

96 "Don't we know each other?" Ibid.

98 "Gone," Ibid.

98 "Come with me . . ." Ibid.

99 "Do you know Christina Kosovska?" Ibid.

100 "Look only forward, you can never look back." Ibid.

100 "Is it true that Zivia was murdered?" Based on Kukiełka, *Underground Wanderings*, 91.

Chapter 14: The Warsaw Ghetto Uprising

101 "The ghetto is surrounded . . ." Lubetkin, *In the Days*, 178.

102 "munitions factory," Meed, *On Both Sides of the Wall*, 135–138. (The original work was published in Yiddish in 1948.)

104 "Look, a woman! A woman fighter!" *Pillar of Fire* (Hebrew version, episode 13). Viewed at Yad Mordechai Museum. Directed by Asher Tlalim. Israel, 1981.

106 "Poles must be fighting alongside the Jews . . ." Kukiełka, *Underground Wanderings*, 94.

Chapter 15: Escape

110 "Responsibility for others brings . . ." Lubetkin, *In the Days*, 236.

110 "It seemed as if you were leaping into the darkness . . ." Ibid., 244.

111 "Let's go back and bring the others!" Ibid., 247.

Chapter 16: Arms, Arms, Arms

114 "I'm responsible . . ." Kukiełka, "The Last Days," *Women in the Ghettos*, 102–106.

114 "But man is made of iron . . ." Ibid.

117 "Powdered paint," Meed, *On Both Sides of the Wall*, 102.

Chapter 17: One Family

121 "I am guilty! Why did I tell them to stay . . ." Kukiełka, *Underground Wanderings*, 98–107.

122 "They shoved us into the train car . . ." Ibid.

122 "I preferred to die this way . . ." Ibid.

123 "After a week of crawling, I arrived here," Ibid.

123 "We are all one family" Ibid.

Chapter 18: Freedom in the Forests

126 "I'd been sitting under a bush . . ." Kukiełka, *Underground Wanderings*, 110–111; Avihu Ronen, *Condemned to Life: The Diaries and Life of Chajka Klinger* [in Hebrew] (Haifa and Tel Aviv, Isr.: University of Haifa Press, Miskal-Yidioth Ahronoth and Chemed, 2011), 295–312.

128 "Why such a serious book?" Rich Cohen, *The Avengers: A Jewish War Story* (New York: Knopf, 2000), 18–19.

129 "I'm just looking for my way home . . ." Ibid.

129 "icy calm" Ibid., 62.

130 "This is not something I felt guilty about . . ." Ibid., 64.

131 "You will have to put a bullet in my head . . ." Ibid., 123.

131 "to borrow a few Jewish girls." Ibid., 125.

133 "You're right," . . . "I am a Jew . . ." Ibid., 140.

133 "It is a miracle that I made it back . . ." Ibid., 142.

Chapter 19: After the Ghettos

138 "live for their family." The discussion about "passing" is from Lenore Weitzman, "Living on the Aryan Side in Poland," *Women in the Holocaust*, eds. Dalia Ofer and Lenore J. Weitzman (New Haven, CT: Yale University Press, 1998), 187–222.

Chapter 20: Missed Connection

141 "Hello," . . . "Are you Antek?" Kukiełka, *Underground Wanderings*, 115.

Chapter 21: Nothing Left to Lose

143 "What's happening?" Kukiełka, *Underground Wanderings*, 118–122.

144 "In my heart I thought: My life has lost all meaning . . ." Ibid.

145 "How did you get here?" Ibid.

145 "Don't cry . . ." Ibid.

145 "My heart wanted to die," Ibid.

Part 3: "No Border Will Stand in Their Way"

147 "They are ready for anything . . ." Chaika Grossman, "For Us the War Has Not Ended," *Women in the Ghettos*, 180–182.

Chapter 22: The Bunker and Beyond

149 "Come to Będzin immediately . . ." Kukiełka, *Underground Wanderings*, 123–124.

152 "I want to breathe my last on the surface . . ." Chajka Klinger, *I am Writing These Words to You: The Original Diaries, Będzin 1943*, trans. Anna Brzostowska and Jerzy Giebułtowski. (Jerusalem, Isr.: Yad Vashem and Moreshet, 2017 [original work published in Hebrew in 2016]), 33–79.

153 "You idiot, calm down . . ." Ibid.

154 "Farewell," Ibid.

155 "Already done!" Ibid.

156 "[The] waiting was worse than death," Ibid.

156 "New faces," . . . "But [okay] . . ." Ibid.

Chapter 23: The Gestapo Net

159 "Please help me," Kukiełka, *Underground Wanderings*, 130–152.

159 "You're Jewish, aren't you?" Ibid.

159 "We should kill you Hebrews, all of you . . ." Ibid.

160 "You're both Polish pigs," Ibid.

160 "She has gray hair, she's elderly . . ." Ibid.

161 "This is the same one as in the previous car," Ibid.

162 "No." Ibid.

163 "I'm Catholic." . . . "The papers are authentic. . . ." Ibid.

164 "No harm will be done to you . . ." Ibid.

164 "No, we can't assume she's Jewish . . ." Ibid.

165 "Do not confess that you are Jewish . . ." Kukiełka video testimony, Yad Vashem archive #4288059, June 20, 2002.

165 "This is the Katowice prison . . ." Kukiełka, *Underground Wanderings*, 143.

166 "Yes, we failed . . ." Ibid.

166 "Wanda Widuchovska!" Ibid., 152.

Chapter 24: The Cuckoo

167 "Go get dressed . . ." Ya'ari-Hazen, *Bronisława Was My Name*, 68–93, and Ya'ari-Hazen's testimony in Dr. M. Dvorshetzky, "From Ghetto to Ghetto," *Women in the Ghettos*, 134–139.

168 "Take a good look at the dress you're wearing . . ." Kukiełka, *Underground Wanderings*, 152–160.

168 "Those people's papers may be fake . . ." Ibid.

168–169 "Everyone who was caught said the same thing . . ." Ibid.

169 "Then you're a spy," Ibid.

169 "If you don't want to talk . . ." Ibid.

169 "Don't you feel it's a waste to die so young? . . ." Ibid.

171 "I think I know you from somewhere," Ya'ari-Hazen, *Bronisława Was My Name*, 68–93.

171 "Is it not enough that I'm suffering? . . ." Ibid.

174 "I'm worried I'll leave you alone . . ." Ibid.

Chapter 25: "Sisters, Revenge!"

176–177 "I never would have thought any human being . . ." Kukiełka, *Underground Wanderings*, 160–173.

177 "Are there any Jews left in Będzin?" Ibid.

178 "Maybe the war will end soon . . ." Ibid.

178 "You are Polish pigs," Ibid.

180 "Let's go." Ibid.

183 "Who stole the gunpowder? Why?" Anna Heilman, *Never Far Away: The Auschwitz Chronicles of Anna Heilman*. (Calgary, Can.: University of Calgary Press, 2001), 79–124.

184 "take care of my sister [Anna] so that I may die easier." Ibid.

184 "Sisters, revenge!" There are different versions of this story, but it appears that Roza called out a cry for vengeance. Ronen Harran. "The Jewish Women at the Union Factory, Auschwitz 1944: Resistance, Courage and Tragedy." *Dapim: Studies in the Holocaust* 31, no. 1 (2017): 59.

Chapter 26: The Light of Days

185 "Any day, someone is going to take you out . . ." Kukiełka, *Underground Wanderings*, 173–179.

186 "I can't tell why I trusted him . . ." Ibid.

186–187 "Two and a half months later, the police arrived . . ." Ibid.

187 "I have a wealthy brother-in-law . . ." Ibid.

188 "That incident awoke my passion for life . . ." Ibid.

Chapter 27: The Great Escape

189 "This is for you . . ." Kukiełka, *Underground Wanderings*, 179–196.

190 "First, you must pay the woman who carried . . ." Ibid.

190 "Everything will be ok . . ." Ibid.

191 "They're acquaintances of a cellmate," Ibid.

191 "It doesn't matter if you fail . . ." Ibid.

192 "No," . . . "You can't go to the fields today." Ibid.

192 "How dare you leave work . . ." Ibid.

193 "So, you're a political prisoner . . ." Ibid.

193 "Come with me, please," Ibid.

196 "They got us!" Ibid.

197 "Renia," . . . "Please keep going. . . ." Ibid.

197 "There's not far left to go," Ibid.

197 "I don't know where she found the strength," Ibid.

198 "as if I was just born." Ibid.

198 "As I started walking away from you, I turned my jacket inside-out . . ." Ibid.

200 "Their fate is mine," Ibid.

200 "Do not," . . . "wait any longer." Ibid.

200 "Get ready for the journey," Ibid.

Chapter 28: The Arrival

207 "She talked for hours and hours . . ." Ronen, *Condemned to Life*, 384–402.

208 "The Hungarians themselves have semitic features . . ." Kukiełka, *Underground Wanderings*, 211.

209 "The situation in Hungary is good for now . . ." Ibid., 212.

209 "Is Madame really Catholic?" Ibid.

210 "They will receive us with open arms . . ." Ibid., 213.

210 "Will our friends in Palestine understand . . ." Ibid., 214.

210–211 "The memory of the millions that were murdered . . ." Ibid.

Part 4: The Emotional Legacy

213 "How are you?" Kukiełka video testimony, Yad Vashem archive #4288059, June 20, 2002.

213 "We had been liberated from the fear of death . . ." Cited in Mordechai Paldiel, *Saving One's Own: Jewish Rescuers in the Holocaust* (Philadelphia and Lincoln: The Jewish Publication Society and University of Nebraska Press, 2017), 394.

Chapter 29: Fear of Life

215 "as if I'd arrived at the home of my parents," Renia Kukiełka testimony, Israel National Library.

215–216 "We felt like we're smaller and weaker . . ." Kukiełka, *Underground Wanderings*, 218.

218 "professional survivors," personal interview, Rivka Augenfeld, Montreal, Canada, August 10, 2018.

218 "the lowest point in my life." Faye Schulman, *A Partisan's Memoir: Warriors of the Holocaust* (Toronto: Second Story Press, 1995), 192.

218 "Never in my life had I felt so lonely . . ." Ibid., 193.

219 "We felt an urgency to proceed quickly . . ." Ibid., 206.

219 "Sometimes [the] bygone world feels almost more real . . ." Ibid., 224.

220 "A mob of people exuberantly rushed out . . ." Lubetkin, *In the Days*, 274.

221 "a circus." Gutterman, *Fighting for Her People*, 361.

222 "catastrophe could hit with no notice." Mira Shelub

and Fred Rosenbaum. *Never the Last Round: A Partisan's Life* (Berkeley, CA: Lehrhaus Judaica, 2015), 174.

Chapter 30: Forgotten Strength

227 "Please take care of my sister Renia," Dawid Liwer, *Town of the Dead: The Extermination of the Jews in the Zaglembie Region* [in Hebrew] (Tel Aviv, Isr.: N. Tverski. 1946), 23.

229 "Life is short," . . . "enjoy everything, appreciate everything." personal interview, Jacob Harel and Leah Waldman, Haifa, Israel, May 14, 2018.

230 "I raised my children and immersed myself in daily life. . . ." Ya'ari-Hazan, *Bronisława Was My Name*, 9–10.

233 "I will live." personal interview, Michael Kovner, Jerusalem, Israel, May 17, 2018.

234 "When she walked into a room . . ." personal interview, Yakov Harel and Leah Waldman, Haifa, Israel, May 14, 2018.

234 "How could someone have gone through what she . . ." personal interview, Merav Waldman, Skype, October 23, 2018.

235 "Family is the most important thing . . ." personal interview, Jacob Harel and Leah Waldman, Haifa, Israel, May 14, 2018.

236 "You always fought like a real hero." Renia's family papers.

FURTHER READING

Bartoletti, Susan Campbell. *Hitler Youth: Growing Up in Hitler's Shadow*. New York: Scholastic, 2005.

Bradley, Kimberly Brubaker. *The War that Saved My Life*. New York: Dial, 2015.

Freeman, Russell. *We Will Not Be Silent: The White Rose Student Resistance Movement That Defied Adolf Hitler*. New York: Clarion Books, 2016.

Gleitzman, Morris. *Once*. New York: Square Fish, 2013.

Golabek, Mona, and Lee Cohen. *The Children of Willesden Lane: A True Story of Hope and Survival During World War II: Young Readers Edition*. New York: Little, Brown and Company for Young Readers, 2017.

Gratz, Alan. *Prisoner B-3087*. New York: Scholastic Press, 2013.

Heiligman, Deborah. *Torpedoed: The True Story of the World War II Sinking of "The Children's Ship."* New York: Henry Holt and Company, 2019.

Lowry, Lois. *Number the Stars.* New York: Sandpiper, 2011.

Mazzeo, Tilar. *Irena's Children: Young Readers Edition, A True Story of Courage.* New York: Margaret K. McElderry Books, 2016.

Opdyke, Irene Gut, with Jennifer Armstrong. *In My Hands: Memories of a Holocaust Rescuer.* New York: Laurel-Leaf Books, 2008.

Warren, Andrea. *Surviving Hitler: A Boy in the Nazi Death Camps.* New York: HarperTrophy, 2002.

Yolen, Jane. *The Devil's Arithmetic.* New York: Puffin, 2005.

Zusak, Markus. *The Book Thief.* New York: Alfred A. Knopf, 2007.

ABOUT THE AUTHOR

Judy Batalion is the *New York Times* bestselling author of the highly-acclaimed *The Light of Days: The Untold Story of Women Resistance Fighters in Hitler's Ghettos*, published by William Morrow in April 2021. *The Light of Days* has been published in a young readers' edition, will be translated into nineteen languages, and has been optioned by Steven Spielberg for a major motion picture for which Judy is cowriting the screenplay. Judy is also the author of *White Walls: A Memoir About Motherhood, Daughterhood and the Mess in Between*, optioned by Warner Bros., and her essays have appeared in the *New York Times*, the *Washington Post*, the *Forward*, *Vogue*, and many other publications. Judy has a BA in the history of science from Harvard and a PhD in the history of art from the Courtauld Institute, University of London, and has worked as a museum curator and university lecturer. Born in Montreal, where she grew up speaking English, French, Hebrew, and Yiddish, she lives in New York with her husband and three children.

www.judybatalion.com

DISCUSSION QUESTIONS

1. How significant was it that Renia was born into a middle-class Jewish family that prioritized education (3)? What advantages did this offer her?

2. Why did the Kukiełka family decide to move to Chmielnik (8)? Why return to Jędrzejów to settle under German rule, instead of pressing forward to freedom (11)?

3. Frumka and Zivia shifted their focus from helping only Freedom members to helping all Jews (17). Why was this important, and did it align with Freedom's values?

4. Why would the Nazis pit Jew against Jew by creating the "Judenrats" (18)? What did the Jewish people who were selected as Judenrat officials hope to achieve?

5. Freedom and other organizations prioritized giving Warsaw ghetto residents access to education, sports opportunities, and theatrical performances (30). Was this an act of resistance? Why, or why not?

6. Why were books so important to Freedom and similar organizations (31)? What was significant about the books and plays that Freedom started to print?

7. What impact did the stories about the Nazis' behavior have on Jewish people living in the Warsaw ghetto (37)? How

did those stories lead to the establishment of the Jewish Fighting Organization?

8. Renia met escapees from a nearby village who were spared by a Nazi soldier after their mother hid them around the house (42). What reason did the Nazi soldier give for sparing their lives?

9. The Nazis rounded up the Jewish people of Będzin and tried to divide them into three lines, but the Jewish people fought back by creating chaos (60). What were some of the other things that the Jews of Będzin did to prevent the Nazis from taking people during the selection? Did their actions help save lives?

10. There were several aspects to Kraków's "Fighting Pioneers" pledge (67). What were some of the ways that it addressed the many types of resistance?

11. How did the uprising at the Warsaw ghetto that was led by the Jewish Fighting Organization (75), challenge the Nazis' perspective of the Jewish people? Why was the effort, which only lasted a short time, considered a success?

12. Renia's role as a *kasharit*, or courier, meant that she was responsible for carrying news (90). Why was Renia's mission of witnessing and reporting the things that were happening to Jewish people so important?

13. Like many of the women who fought in the resistance, Zivia felt a great deal of guilt for the comrades that she

wasn't able to save (109). How did emotional trauma play a role in Zivia's actions during the war, and how did it impact the rest of her life?

14. The couriers were able to smuggle weapons, bribe officers, and meet secret contacts (116). How did they use their gender to avoid suspicion?

15. Chajka befriended German soldiers in Będzin and told them about the horrific things that were happening to the Jewish people (157). Why did she do that, and what impact did she hope to have?

16. Bela and Lonka were able to reconnect after they were both captured and brought to the Pawiak prison (171). Why was it dangerous for Jewish women to identify each other when they were imprisoned in jails or at concentration camps?

17. Gusta wrote her memoirs using scraps of toilet paper sewn together with thread (195). Was that an act of resistance? Why?

18. Renia worried that Jewish people in Palestine wouldn't be able to understand what European Jews went through in the Holocaust (210). Why was this a concern? How did the lack of understanding impact the way the couriers and resistance fighters assimilated into the new land?

19. How were the women like Faye Schulman (218), who spoke publicly about their experiences during the war, still participating in the resistance even after the war was over?

20. What were some of the reasons that it was hard for women like Zivia (220) to adjust to post-war life?

21. What was the brigade of the Avengers (233) hoping to achieve by continuing their work after the war?